ONE WEEK LOAN

ISRAEL'S AYATOLLAHS

Meir Kahane and
the Far Right in Israel

ISRAEL'S AYATOLLAHS

Meir Kahane and
the Far Right in Israel

Raphael Mergui
& Philippe Simonnot

Saqi Books

British Library
Cataloguing in Publication Data
Mergui, Raphael
   Israel's ayatollahs : Meir Kahane and
   the far right in Israel.
   1. Conservatism—Israel 2. Israel—
   Politics and government
   I. Title II. Simonnot, Philippe III. Meir,
   Kahane : le Rabbin qui fait peur aux
   Juifs. *English*
   320.95694   JQ1825.P37

   ISBN 0 86356 142 X
        0 86356 054 7 Pbk

Library of Congress
Cataloging-in-Publication data
   LC 87-9884

First published as
Meir Kahane: le rabbin qui fait peur aux juifs
by Editions Pierre-Marcel Favre, Lausanne, 1985.
© Pierre-Marcel Favre, Publi SA.

This edition first published 1987.
Saqi Books, 26 Westbourne Grove, London W2 5RH
and 171 First Avenue, Atlantic Highlands, NJ 07716

Contents

I
The Pariah

The name of Rabbi Meir Kahane★ provokes strong reactions both inside and outside of Israel. ★ We wanted to find out why. At first we expected to find a self-styled Messiah★ peddling cheap slogans, but we discovered that his seemingly simplistic slogans were the fruits of a thought-out and well-argued dialectic. Can a state be simultaneously Jewish and secular? In other words, are Judaism and democracy compatible? Not in the opinion of this strange rabbi who is prepared to say out loud that he is no democrat, and that the Jewish state can only survive if it drives all Arabs out of Israel. How is it that his ideas have generated such a following? Simply because the Jewish state has no answer to the problem that is so vital for its future existence: what to do with its Arabs, be they citizens or simply under its 'administration'.

The intelligence — some would call it cunning — of this outcast of Judaism is that he has found a brash new language in which to pose a question that is as old as the Diaspora, ★ a question that concerns us all: what is a Jew? Paradoxically, this rabbi thought that he would scare the Arabs. Instead he frightens the Jews. Almost a 'Jewish joke'.

We have listened very carefully to Rabbi Kahane — a former FBI agent, a professional agitator, the instigator of an anti-Soviet terror network, a man who for a while had connections with the American Mafia, an ardent baseball fan, head of a political party, and now a member of the Israeli parliament. What he told us went a long way to explain the basic facts of the tragedy in the Middle East, facts which are of such crucial importance to the future of world peace.

However, before we can understand why Kahane's brash utterances have become such a nightmare for the state of Israel, we have to view them in the context of the growth of the Israeli extreme Right, and the religious and pioneer fever which is taking such a grip on the country's disoriented youth.

NB: We have included a glossary of Hebrew words, names of organizations, etc. An asterisk in the text denotes the first reference to each item that is glossed.

1
From the FBI
to the Knesset

Meir Kahane wears the Orthodox *yarmulka*★ and beard. He is a practising Jew, a believer. More to the point, he is also a rabbi. Unusually elegant for an Israeli, wearing a jacket and open-necked shirt, with his lean figure and brisk, swinging gait he does not look his 53 years. Meir Kahane is a baseball fan and a keen supporter of the Dodgers. He is unmistakably American, and speaks with the characteristic accent of a Brooklyn Jew.

He has a way with words, the streetwise humour of a kid raised in New York's rougher back streets, and this has given him the ability to accept insults with a smile, and to defend even his most indefensible ideas with a strange serenity. Meir Kahane is a fanatic, yet he is also self-confident, almost placid.

Once in a while, the fine-lined features of his face are disturbed by a nervous twitch. Serenity too has its price. His admirers see in him a Joshua★ leading the Israelites in the conquest of the Promised Land — only this time from West to East — or an Ezra seeking to 'purify' the Jewish people; the more moderate of his critics see him as a militarist adventurer à la Bar Kokhba, ★ or a false Messiah; his opponents, by far the majority, simply call him Adolf Kahane. Meir Kahane takes his inspiration from Moses: 'When Moses saw the Egyptians beat a Jew,' he says, 'he did not found a committee to investigate the roots of anti-

Semitism... ' He argues — with some justification — that the Bible does not forbid 'killing' but 'assassination'. Action, constant action is what moves him. And that includes terrorism.

What about his political beliefs? Israel and the Jews are a pariah state and a pariah people *par excellence*. 'Israel', he writes, 'has a great talent, a great ability to reconcile the worst of enemies and to create a united, universal human society. What other state has the power to reconcile the USSR and China, Vietnam and Cambodia, Egypt and Libya, Muslims and Christians, Blacks, Whites, Browns, Yellows, the first, second, third and twelfth world, fascists and communists? Hatred for the Jewish state brings universal unity in an otherwise divided world.'

And the crux of his politics? To change the Declaration of Independence★ which defines Israel as both a Jewish and a secular state: 'The schizophrenic Jew has both legs firmly planted in... a vacuum. He says that Israel is a Jewish state which the Arabs have the right to change into something else by democratic means!' By letting the Arabs believe that they can be equal to the Jews in a Jewish state, Zionism★ is an 'insult to their intelligence'. From this, two conclusions follow: first, if the Arabs cannot be equal to the Jews and if Israel does not want to become another Ireland or South Africa, then the Arabs must be expelled. Second, if the state is to be a Jewish state, no one has yet found any justification for its existence other than religion. And where does democracy fit into all this? It is a Western value, completely foreign to the spirit of Judaism...

David Meir Kahane was born in the Flatbush district of Brooklyn in 1932. His grandfather had been a rabbi in Palestine. His father, also a rabbi, emigrated to the United States. In 1947, at the age of 15, Meir Kahane committed his first act of violence, hurling tomatoes at the British minister Ernest Bevin, to protest against the internment of Jewish refugees in Cyprus. This led to the first in a long series of arrests.

He was ordained rabbi by a New York seminary in 1955; two years later, he was expelled by the small congregation whose spiritual head he had become, for excessive religious zeal.

Meir Kahane decided not to push the point. He turned to studying law and international relations, but failed to qualify for the New York bar. He returned from a visit to Israel in 1963 showing no particular enthusiasm for the country. As a rabbi without a congregation, a lawyer without a practice, and a disappointed Zionist, Kahane was free and available. His anti-communist views opened doors at the FBI, where he was hired under the name of Michael King. His job was to infiltrate the John Birch Society, an American organization known for its extreme right-wing and anti-Semitic views. Kahane is still proud of this episode in his life, although his association with the FBI has definitely made him suspect in the eyes of many of his opponents, who tend to see him as an agent of the CIA.

During the Vietnam War, Kahane, still using the name Michael King, devoted his militant energies to waging war on the pacifists. His attempts to be accepted among anti-communist circles in Washington, however, met with little success. He set up a 'Research Center' and a mysterious 'Fourth of July Movement'. This period saw the publication of a book with the curious title *The Jewish Venture in Vietnam*, co-authored by Messrs Churba, Kahane and Michael King! The financial backers of this operation remain unknown. In 1967, Kahane found a more honourable position, as editor-in-chief of America's largest Jewish newspaper, the *Jewish Press*. But he felt uneasy among the Jewish establishment, of whom he was to write: 'They breathe guilt the way other people breathe oxygen.'

The 'little Jews' of Brooklyn, a hotbed of racial tensions at this time, were of the same opinion. They accused their rich co-religionists of being more generous with the Blacks than with their own brothers. Among them, Meir Kahane at last found the field of battle he had been seeking. Bidding farewell to journalism, he decided to put himself at the service of those whom he considered the pariahs of American Judaism.

Encouraged by Israel's lightning victory in 1967, he began organizing Jewish self-defence patrols. Run-ins with the black population were becoming a daily event. The Jewish Defense League (JDL), founded by himself and a lawyer friend, Bertram Zweidon, included a paramilitary organization. The young recruits had to undergo rough training in camps located in the Catskill Mountains: martial arts, target practice, bomb-making, etc. Stickers proclaiming 'Every Jew his .22' (ie .22 rifle) began to appear on car bumpers in the locality.

But the Jewish–Black conflicts in Brooklyn did not last, and Kahane was to find a new cause to espouse: the defence of the Jews in Russia. He declared war on Soviet diplomats in Washington and New York, with the stated aim of provoking conflict between the USSR and the United States, so that, as he said, 'the problem of the Russian Jews becomes Nixon's problem'.

There was a sudden increase in bomb attacks on Soviet cars and buildings. Responsibility for them was always claimed by an anonymous caller who would shout down the phone: 'Never Again!', the slogan of the JDL. On each occasion, Kahane denied having instigated these attacks, but he 'applauded' them enthusiastically.

He aroused the hostility of the Jewish community, who excluded him from their World Conference in Brussels in 1971. The Belgian government followed suit by banishing him from the country. The rabbi had rather more luck with the American Mafia. In 1971, he entered into a strange alliance with the 'League for the Civil Rights of Italo-Americans', which served as a respectable front for one of the New York family heads, Joe Colombo.

By this time, the JDL claimed to have over 14,000 members throughout the United States, Canada, Britain and the Netherlands, many of them former leftist students. Kahane decided that the League could now do without him. At the end of 1971, he emigrated to Israel, with his wife and four children. There he found a new enemy: the Arabs.

In fact he was to divide his time between Israel and the United States. No sooner had he settled in Jerusalem, on 14 September, than he was summoned back to New York to stand trial for 'illegal transport of arms' and 'harassment of the Soviet mission in the United States'. He confessed to having made bombs, and was given a five-year suspended prison sentence.

The sentence seemed to trigger off new energies in Kahane. His plotting continued, and led to several arrests. He fought relentlessly on both the Russian and the Arab 'fronts'. His everyday life involved him in arms smuggling and bombings which often had tragic consequences. There were also moments of tragicomedy.

In April 1971, the headquarters of AMTORG, the USSR's commercial mission in New York, were bombed. A few minutes later, another bomb was discovered and defused in the nick of time. It would have cost the life of Albert Seedman, the guard on duty, who, as it turned out, was a Jew. In a later episode, JDL militants fired shots at a bedroom window in the Soviet mission to the United Nations, almost killing four children. Needless to say, the windows of the Aeroflot offices on 49th Street did not escape their attentions either.

On occasion, Kahane used less injurious means to 'make life impossible for the Russians', as he puts it. At a Young Communists Congress in Israel, he pretended to be a foreign reporter and sprayed the Soviet delegation with Coca Cola. Touring Russian artistes provided another suitable target. A group of JDL activists interrupted a concert by Soviet musicians by releasing mice into the concert hall. This had the frightened spectators jumping up onto their seats. Similarly, at the Carnegie Hall in New York, the Omsk Choir had just started its performance when people started to throw bottles of ammonia and forced the choir to interrupt its singing. Shortly afterwards, the Bolshoi Ballet cancelled its planned tour of the United States. Kahane, for whom these performances were far from politically innocuous, was delighted.

But the League were not just a bunch of pranksters. As it turned out, their anti-Soviet phobia was to prove their downfall. By this time, the American government was waking up to the fact that the turbulent rabbi had to be taken more seriously. George Bush, at that time US ambassador to the United Nations, mobilized the FBI, the secret service, the attorney-general, the Justice Department and the police to keep a close eye on Kahane and his followers. Their efforts were soon to be rewarded.

In a cellar in Boro Park, New York, a group of JDL sympathizers were building a radio-controlled plane with a six-foot wingspan. Loaded with six sticks of TNT, this flying bomb was to be controlled from a car cruising along Park Avenue, and its target was to have been the Soviet Embassy to the United Nations.

By this time, the police were on the trail of the AMTORG terrorists, and the bomb's high-precision timing mechanism led them to a DIY genius, 26-year-old Sheldon Seigal. Sergeant Santo Parola did not arrest the young man; instead, he 'converted' him, and the militant League member turned police informer.

Since they were now forewarned, the police were able to prevent the planting of a bomb in a Soviet diplomat's car and the firing of a mortar shell against a Soviet-owned building at Glen Cove, New York. A plot to assassinate Soviet ambassador Anatole Dobrynin was similarly nipped in the bud. More importantly, though, the booby-trap plane was definitively grounded.

Seigal, however, turned out to be an unreliable informer. Not only did he stop informing the police, he also started spying on them. Two bombs exploded in the centre of Manhattan without the police getting advance notice. The first devastated the offices of the Columbia Artists organization which was organizing the tours of Soviet artists. Nobody was hurt.

At the same time, a bomb concealed in an attaché-case was left in the 56th Street offices of the Jewish impresario Sol Hurok, who was arranging a tour for the Osipov Balalaika Orchestra. Hurok and two of his employees survived the blast with shock, but his young Jewish secretary was killed, asphyxiated by the fumes. Kahane, who was in Jerusalem at the time of the tragedy, denied all responsibility, but Seigal disclosed the names of two important members of the JDL. One of them, Stuart Cohen,* the JDL's spokesperson, had been recruited by Kahane, who had been his philosophy teacher at the Yeshiva* High School in the Queens district of New York. The other, Sheldon Davis, had initially intended to sign up as a professional soldier, but Kahane had convinced him to put his military inclinations at the service of the JDL. Seigal, Cohen and Davis were charged with the murder of Iris Kones on 16 June 1972.

The trial took place in New York, in decidedly strange circumstances. Judge Arnold Bauman, defence lawyers Barry I. Slotnik, Bertram Zweidon and Alan Dershowitz, the two prosecutors Henry L. Putzell III and Joseph Jaffé, as well as the three defendants, were all Jewish. But the surprising acquittal of Seigal, Cohen and Davis was not due to this concidence. They were acquitted because Sergeant Santo Parola had obtained evidence of their guilt by illegal means: phone-tapping and a non-authorized search of Seigal's car. Though irrefutable, the evidence was inadmissable in court. It was with a heavy heart that Judge

Bauman had to acquit the three men, although he closed the case with these words: 'They have committed a crime that is inexcusable, unforgettable...'

US justice finally caught up with Kahane in 1975. Without waiting out his five-year suspended sentence, Kahane had called on members of the League to kill or kidnap Soviet ambassadors and to bomb the Iraqi Embassy in Washington.

This time, he was sentenced to one year's imprisonment, which he served... in a hotel in Manhattan. He was free to move about as he wished, and ate his meals in restaurants at the expense of the US government. Kahane had managed to convince Judge Jack Weinstein that it would have been unconstitutional to send him to the state penitentiary in Allenwood, Pennsylvania, since they did not serve kosher meals. Consequently, being 'in prison' did not keep the rabbi from continuing his activities: he held press conferences and met freely with other members of the League.

Iris Kones' death effectively marked the end of this phase of anti-Soviet terror. The League had not killed a single Soviet citizen. Kahane, however, believes that he had achieved his objective: the tragedy of the Russian Jews became known worldwide, and was now making headline news.

The assassination of the eleven Israeli athletes in Munich in 1972 marked a further turning point in Kahane's eventful life. From now on, his activities were directed almost exclusively against Arabs. He started organizing large-scale, worldwide arms deals in order to 'defend the Jews of the Diaspora against the Arabs'. According to Kahane, 'the Jews serve as a target all over the world because of Israel'. Yet neither Israel nor the Jewish establishment supported them. In a book published during that same year, Kahane derided the American Jews who were peacefully surfing along the beaches of Miami on the eve of World War II, while a few miles away their German co-religionists were being expelled from Havana and had to wander from port to port in search of a safe berth.

On 21 September 1972, Kahane issued a clear public appeal: 'There is only one solution to Arab terror — Jewish counter-terror.' He claimed to have a large number of volunteers, among them former members of the Irgun★ and Stern★ groups.

No sooner had he started on his new activities than he was arrested. The police discovered an arms cache consisting of grenades and explosives in the grounds of Tel Aviv airport on 6 October 1972. Kahane had intended to smuggle them to the United States, to be used against Soviet and Arab diplomats. He was released on $10,000 bail. One of his associates met a similar fate when he tried to smuggle arms onto a British plane leaving Kennedy airport, to be used in hijacking an Egyptian plane to Tel Aviv. The aborted operations are known; the many successful ones are not. Nor is it known whether Kahane and his followers played a part in the tit-for-tat killings between Israelis and Palestinians in Europe during the 1970s.

Kahane's record in Israel was equally newsworthy. According to an Israeli police officer, Kahane and his American followers had come to Israel to play 'cowboys and Indians'. In October 1972, Kahane was arrested for having tried to fix a *mezuzah*★ onto the Damascus Gate in Jerusalem, to set a claim to the Old City as 'Jewish property'. Called up to do his military service as a reservist on the West Bank, Kahane captured so many Arab 'suspects' in one day that he was suspended forthwith. Israeli intelligence services at this time attributed a number of 'semi-professional' terrorist attacks on Arabs to the Kach party which Kahane had just founded — *kach* (pronounced as the German 'ach') being the Hebrew for 'thus it is'.

Rabbi Kahane openly approved of the armed attacks on the West Bank Arab mayors in 1980. In March 1982, one of his American followers, Harry Goldman, killed two

Arabs in the Old City of Jerusalem. Others machine-gunned a Palestinian bus near Ramallah. Kach also 'approved' of the killing of students at the Islamic University of Hebron.

In early 1984, the mysterious group TNT (Terror Against Terror) was formed. It took credit for an attack on a bus in Jerusalem in which four people were killed. Members of the Kach party were arrested. TNT was suspected of being the armed wing of the Kach party, but no evidence for this has yet been forthcoming. In November 1984, David Ben-Shimol fired a shell at an Arab bus; his deed was promptly celebrated by Kahane, who made him an 'honorary member' of Kach. Yehuda Richter, number two on the Kach electoral list, was arrested on suspicion of having actively participated in these terrorist acts. Kahane himself was taken into custody more than a dozen times in Israel, but was never sentenced, due to lack of evidence.

He owed his longest period of detention, in 1980, to Ezer Weizman, then defence minister and minister in charge of security in the Occupied Territories. He was released after thirty days of 'administrative detention', thanks to the personal intervention of Menachem Begin — not that Begin had any particular liking for Kahane.

As long as he could be seen as a religious eccentric, Rabbi Kahane alarmed no one, especially since he had twice failed to be elected to the Knesset,* in 1977 and in 1981. But when, in the July 1984 elections, he obtained 25,000 votes — 1.2 per cent of the total vote — the effect in Israel was that of a political earthquake. The Central Election Committee had tried to outlaw the Kach party, but was overruled by the Supreme Court. The Committee's reasons are nevertheless worth noting: 'The Kach movement is motivated by racist and anti-democratic concepts; it publicly supports terrorist activities; it stirs up rancour and hatred between different sections of the population, casts aspersions on the religious feelings of particular sections of the community, and undermines the very foundations of democracy in Israel.'

Haim Herzog refused to receive Kahane after the elections. Never before in the history of Israel had a head of state refused to receive a party leader. As for Rabbi Kahane, he felt proud to have become the pariah of Israeli politics. In a way, it suits his temperament.

On the extreme Right, the head of the movement for 'Greater Israel', Yuval Neeman, also refused an official meeting. Rabbi Moshe Levinger, leader of the Gush Emunim ('Bloc of the Faithful'), the main colonizing movement on the West Bank, believes him to be a dangerous man. Not only is Kahane rejected by his own political family; he is also an object of contempt among the big parties. Yitzhak Shamir, head of the Likud party, openly disavows him: 'The Kahane phenomenon is negative, detrimental and dangerous.'

In the left-wing camp, Prime Minister Shimon Peres declares laconically: 'Each country has its fascists.' Shevah Weiss, a Labour Party MP and university academic, sums up the sense of shame felt by liberal Israelis: 'Meir Kahane is without doubt a fascist; the only difference between his followers and the Hitler Youth is the colour of their shirts. We definitely have a fascist list represented in the parliament of the Jewish state.'

Jerusalem's mayor Teddy Kollek asked the Knesset to pass a bill against racism. Many Israelis feel that they are living a reverse version of the things that they themselves have suffered. Kahane is seen as a Jewish reincarnation of Hitler; his programme is compared to the Nuremberg Laws. One commentator has even suggested that Haim Herzog is perhaps Israel's von Hindenburg... Those Israelis who cannot believe that such a thing as a fascist Jew can exist are inclined to believe that Kahane has been set up by the Arabs with the express intention of embarrassing

the Hebrew state. A special law now exists, barring Kahane
from making speeches in schools.

Followers of the Kach party, wearing yellow T-shirts
decorated with a clenched fist, had barely ended their march
through the Old City of Jerusalem to celebrate Kahane's
election in 1984 when a group of young Israelis distributed
leaflets to the Arab population apologizing for Kahane's
behaviour.

On 30 July 1984, the Chief Rabbinate of Israel implicitly
condemned Kahane, by citing the words of the highly
venerated Israeli rabbi Abraham Yitzhak Kuk, who had
advocated a 'fraternal relationship with the Arab population'. Kahane, however, overstepped the mark. Hiding
behind his newly acquired parliamentary immunity, he
decided to go to the villages of the 'Galilee Triangle', which
are mainly inhabited by Israeli Arabs, to 'encourage them
to emigrate'. Despite his immunity, the police finally
arrested him in September at Umm el-Fahm, and in
October at Taibeh. On each occasion, left-wing Israelis
mobilized in solidarity with the Arabs. A number of rabbis
also spent the Sabbath★ with the Arab population in order
to demonstrate their solidarity with them.

On 25 December 1984, the Knesset reacted by partially
revoking Kahane's parliamentary immunity — an unusual
measure in self-styled hyperdemocratic Israel. His freedom
of movement in areas populated by Arabs was restricted;
should he venture to visit these areas, he was to be treated
like an ordinary citizen. Still, about thirty-six members of
parliament voted against this measure, and others contrived
to be absent on the day of the vote, not necessarily because
they approved of Kahane's conduct, but because they considered it a dangerous precedent in a country where members of parliament are granted freedoms of action and
movement unheard of in other countries.

Once more, Kahane was delighted to have stirred public
interest. A few days later, he repeated the offence by going

to Hebron in order to 'celebrate' the fact that the Palestinian leader Fahd Qawasmeh had been assassinated in Amman. He locked himself into his car to escape arrest, but the police smashed the windows, pulled him out and took him back to Jerusalem. Rabbi Kahane had won: he made the front pages of the Israeli press, and his action aroused editorial comment around the world.

This publicity served to reinforce the rabbi's political position in Israel. His stock with the electorate went up, and an opinion poll published in December 1984 gave him an estimated 2.6 per cent of the vote — equivalent to three seats in the Knesset.

The sense of horror which Kahane arouses in the great majority of Israeli and Diaspora Jews is genuine. Politicians in Israel are sincere when they condemn him outright. In some cases, however, their strong aversion to the 'Kahane phenomenon' seems to be coloured by ulterior political motives, which often lead onto contradictory ground.

The effect of Meir Kahane's radicalism is to confer an aura of respectability on the extreme Right. By an irony of history, he is pushing the Likud to the centre Right of the political chessboard. But both the extreme Right and the Right realize that Kahane has drawn, and will be drawing, votes from among their own supporters. Therefore they owe it to themselves to condemn him, while at the same time supporting his views... A dangerous enterprise! Likud and the small 'expansionist' parties want to annex the West Bank but not its Arab population; they would prefer to keep them as foreign residents, a solution that is likely to bring explosive outbreaks of racial and religious conflict. Kahane pushes the positions of the 'National Unity' camp (Likud and the extreme Right) to their logical limit, and his theses have the advantage of simplicity. His intention of driving out the Arabs is not only logical. It also expresses the secret views of a minority of politicians and of 'clever' generals who dream of a 'soft' expulsion of the Arabs, or an exodus provoked by an armed conflict for which Israel's neighbouring countries would bear the responsibility. Thus, for a minority of his apparent opponents, Kahane's mistake is not that he wants to get rid of the Arabs, but that he says so publicly and lacks patience.

The Left, for its part, has nothing to fear from the Kach electorally. But Kahane still represents a fundamental challenge to them. If we exclude its notorious doves, the Labour camp believes that, for strategic reasons, it cannot give up the whole of the West Bank and the Gaza Strip. For them, if a solution is possible, it has to lie in a sharing of territories with Jordan (which in fact would not solve the problem of the status of the West Bank's Palestinian population). The Labour Party has never clearly defined its position on this. Wavering between the two poles of a contradiction — their desire to keep at least part of the Occupied Territories, and their desire to maintain both the Jewish and the democratic features of Israel — they have no clear answers to this problem that is so vitally important for Israel's future. Granted, Shimon Peres is a pragmatist, and pragmatism is a wonderful thing. But it is hard to apply it when you are governing the People of the Book, and your country is racked by doubt. The danger of 'Kahanism' is that it could easily exacerbate and strengthen Palestinian nationalism in the Occupied Territories. The ruling Left is not sure that it has the political means to stop this trend.

But that is not all. The Labour Party itself is not immune to dreams of depopulating the Occupied Territories. On 15 January 1980, the *Jerusalem Post* published a letter which reminded readers that in 1937 Golda Meir had demanded from the Zionist Congress a transfer to neighbouring states of the Arab population then living on the territory of the future state of Israel (*New Judea*, August/September 1937); and that even more recently the *Christian Science Monitor* of 3 January 1974, and the *Yediot Aharanot* of 23 July, published Rabin's proposal that the Arabs of the Gaza Strip and the West Bank emigrate to the eastern borders of the Jordan river.

The roots of Kach are not only political. They are sociological and ideological too. Meir Kahane recruits his most fervent supporters from among repentant leftists, often North Americans, in search of a new area of involvement. At party gatherings, these sloppy young men in jeans and sneakers meet with formally dressed, crisp little men — Russians — who have brought from the USSR a bad habit of liking politicians who give clear-cut, simple answers.

The people who merely give Kahane their votes are quite a different matter. These are the poor, the Oriental Jews, who are not easily impressed with the dull rhetoric of the socialist aristocracy. To be precise, we can say that it is the not so well-off Sephardis* of the lower social classes, the outcasts of Israeli society, who have taken Kahane most to heart. He took 33 per cent of his vote from development towns,* 33 per cent from the religious *moshavim*,* and 23 per cent from the poorer sections of the large cities — all areas inhabited by Oriental Jews; 2.5 per cent of Jews of Oriental origin voted for him, and 0.4 per cent of European Jews. By way of comparison, Arie Eliav, ex-secretary of Mapai* and a well-known dove, who devotes all his time to the 'rehabilitation' of Sephardis and who has lived among them for many years, obtained only 0.4 per cent of their votes.

The same phenomenon occurred in the armed forces: Kahane's support in the armed forces was double what it was in the country as a whole. For the young generation now voting for Kahane, it makes no more sense to differentiate between the 'Green Line' (1967) border and present-day frontiers than it did for their parents to differentiate between the borders of the 1947 partition plan and the enlarged Israel of 1949.

Kahane is the product of Israeli society. But he is also

a product of Arab extremism. Israeli liberals wait impatiently for the emergence of a Palestinian *Shalom Akhshav*★ ('Peace Now') movement which would unreservedly and unambiguously recognize the state of Israel, and would aid them in their struggle for peaceful coexistence between Israelis and Palestinians. A liberal Jew has written: 'One has to apologize twice: once for Kahane and Sabra and Chatila, and also for all your left-wing friends throughout the world who join their voices with those of the anti-Zionists. To be a Jew today inevitably turns you into a cynic, because the slightest *faux pas* by the Israelis is put under the microscope and examined, and raises a storm far greater than the Iran–Iraq war, which is more of a killer than Hiroshima and Nagasaki put together.'

Since winning a seat in the Knesset, Kahane appears to have 'calmed down' a little. Take, for example, the statement he made during our interview with him — that violence has to be in proportion to popular support. It would be no surprise if one day Kahane too found himself overtaken on the right.

2
God's Law:
an Interview
with Rabbi Meir Kahane

*Question: Rabbi Meir Kahane, you have been politically active
for many years, but only in 1984 were you able to win a seat in
the Knesset. Compared to your objectives, is this not rather a
disappointing result?*

Answer: Tens of thousands would have liked to vote for
me. If they didn't, it's either because they were afraid to,
or because they thought that I had no chance of winning.
But at the next elections, it would be a mistake to think
that I'll only have four seats. I'll have double that.

From the start we have addressed ourselves to the
Sephardic Jews. These people have lived among the Arabs.
They know what Arabs are. They have no racist complexes. And they tell themselves that I know how to deal
with their problems. The next time, every young Sephardi,
especially those living in the development towns, will vote
for Kahane.

*Q: But people say that the young Sephardis, since they come
from Arab countries, know nothing about democracy. That they
are backward. And your success will depend on the votes of these
backward people!*

A: This is an arrogant comment, typical of European
intellectuals. This really is nothing but intellectualism. The
Sephardic Jew is an intelligent Jew. Thank God, the

Sephardis are not spoiled by European culture. Thank God! They have not been corrupted by the teachings of college professors.

Q: But aren't they Arabic, in culture?

A: The Sephardis came to this country with a culture, which is Judaism. But here their family structures have been shattered; their morale has been destroyed. Theirs is not an Arab culture. It's a true Jewish culture. So, when a Sephardi says that he is against Western democracy, he knows what he is talking about.

Q: How do you see Western democracy?

A: First I'm going to give you a bit of background, to help you understand. Among all the controversy surrounding Kahane you'll not find anybody prepared to take up the challenge that I have thrown down. Since people are not capable of debating, they attack me by putting labels on me. The first thing I want to say is that I couldn't care less what they call me, and that's what makes them so mad. The Left has always acted that way when they want to attack the Right. The problem is that these people don't know how to debate. Let's get to the point. First you must understand that Zionism and Western democracy are at odds. And according to Zionism, this country must be a Jewish state.

Q: What exactly is a Jewish state?

A: A Jewish state means that, at a minimum, there must be a majority of Jews; a Jewish sovereignty with the power to make our own laws. This is why Jews have left Europe and have come here. If we were now to apply to the letter the principles of Western democracy, we would have to agree that decisions are to be made by a majority. It's at this point that I ask a question that sends Israelis crazy, both on the Left and on the Right. The question is as follows: if the Arabs settle among us and make enough children to become a majority, will Israel continue to be a Jewish state? Do we have to accept that the Arab majority will decide? Obviously, nobody in Israel can accept this. Because to accept this would amount to being anti-Zionist!

Q: Would you accept a situation in which there was democracy only for the Jews and not for the Arabs?

A: I'll answer that question later. First let me explain why everybody is mad at me. It's because I have confronted people with the following contradiction: you can't have Zionism and democracy at the same time. And for those who criticize me, it's very difficult to get out of this contradiction.

Now let me answer your question. First of all, Western democracy has to be ruled out. For me that's cut and dried: there's no question of setting up democracy in Israel, because democracy means equal rights for all, irrespective of racial or religious origins. Therefore democracy and Zionism cannot go together. And Israel's Declaration of Independence, which proclaimed this state to be a Jewish state, is a totally schizophrenic document. You just can't, on the one hand, want a Jewish state and at the same time give non-Jews the right to become a majority. When Abba Eban makes beautiful speeches in twelve languages and starts talking about Jewish democracy — what on earth does that mean, Jewish democracy?

Let's get back to your question and let me talk about democracy as far as Jews are concerned. Do I accept democracy for Judaism? My answer is: Judaism does not accept democracy unless it is within a structure that adheres to the law of the Torah. ★ I challenge any rabbi to contradict me on this. My hope as a religious Jew, which is the hope of every sincere and religious Jew, is to have a state governed by the Torah. If one accepts the commandments of the Torah, then democracy is conceivable within the framework of those commandments. Of course, nobody could vote against these commandments. Nobody could question the fact that the government has to abide by the Torah. There is no question of letting people vote for or against the commandments of the Torah. This can't be decided by a vote. However, if this objective cannot be reached without having a civil war in Israel, then I'd give it up. Therefore I hope that we'll be able to convince a majority of Jews to create a state governed by the Torah, and that the minority will accept it. And then, if that means voting in elections every four years so as to have a government in compliance with the Torah, of course I'd accept it. But I can't say that I'd be pleased with it.

Q: Concretely, what kind of constitution would this state have?

A: Who says that a state must have a constitution?

Q: All right then, let's talk about institutions.

A: In a state governed by the Torah, there must be a king, or if not a king, then a president. But the supreme authority must lie with a rabbinic court. The supreme laws of the country must be established by that court. I guess there could also be a parliament to take care of certain things, such as the army, or prisons. If the rules concerning the army or the prisons are not contrary to the Torah, there would be no problem.

However, obviously, the supreme law is the Halacha★ and it must be interpreted by the Supreme Rabbinic Court, which is the Sanhedrin.★ Applying the Halacha would entail great differences with the present situation. Respecting the Sabbath, for example, would be compulsory. All driving around in cars would be banned on the Sabbath. Obviously, you wouldn't have a secret police force going round to people's homes to check whether they eat kosher★ food or not. But kosher food would have to be compulsory in all public places such as restaurants.

And that leads me to the second thing that drives my opponents crazy. The biggest racist is the Jew who doesn't see that to be a Jew is something special. When I say that I am a Jew, it means that I accept that there is a wall separating Jews and non-Jews. It's a terrible thing to create a wall between people — between Jews and non-Jews in this case. But this is conceivable when there are reasons to be Jewish and to want to live one's Jewishness. But for a secular Zionist, what reasons could he have, other than a point of view that is basically racist?

No secular Zionist in this country can quietly sit down and listen to his son telling him: 'Dad, I've met a great girl...' If that woman is not Jewish, no secular Zionist is going to tell him: 'Son, don't marry her.' He would be called a racist pig. But under these conditions, what's going to become of us? There would no longer be any reason to be Jewish. The only thing that distinguishes us from non-Jews is that we have the Torah. That's all. We are not superior to others. The Chinese are intelligent too. There are stupid Jews. There are intelligent Jews. Other peoples may also have their Einstein. The biggest racism would be to create a Jewish state that isn't Jewish, that has no reason for being. Without that reason of being Jewish, why create a Jewish state? Without that reason, why be a Jew and not just a human being?

I believe that there is a God and that this God led us into Sinai and revealed the Truth to us. This is the reason that makes one a Jew.

Q: This state ruled by the Torah would not guarantee freedom of speech, then?

A: Of course not! In a religious state, there can be no such freedom.

Obviously, I think that today it is not possible for us to have such a state without a civil war, and I'm not prepared to encourage such a conflict. What I am ready for, though, is to tell my voters that I want a religious state. And if the people vote for me, then we'll have the religious state that

I'm hoping for. And if, four years later, at the next elections, they no longer want a religious state, they can vote against it.

My worst nightmare is to see Jews fighting other Jews.

Q: In this Jewish state, would you apply biblical punishments, such as the death penalty for incest or adultery?

A: The Halacha provides for a death penalty only if there is a Sanhedrin. Without a Sanhedrin, the Halacha does not allow capital punishment. And in present-day Israel there is no Sanhedrin. Therefore there cannot be a death penalty.

Q: In a religious state, will all public schools have to be religious?

A: If someone wants to send his children to a private school, he's free to open a private school.

But in a religious Jewish state, all public schools will have to be religious. It's through education that I want to achieve my objectives. What I want is not at all the Western state that some people would like to see. There are many rights which Western democracy considers fundamental and which I consider to be without foundation.

Q: What rights?

A: For example, the right not to respect the Sabbath. This right must not exist. In all public life, the Sabbath will have to be respected. Restaurants must be kosher. If you don't want to eat kosher food, you'll just have to eat at home. As for censorship, it already exists in Western democracies, and in the state that I want to see, there will obviously be censorship. The atmosphere in which this country lives must change.

Q: Will the members of that Supreme Rabbinic Court be elected by the citizens?

A: No. Very much not so. This is out of the question. The judges will have to be nominated, not elected.

Q: But supposing that the rabbis in this court don't agree with each other. If Israel is not to become a totalitarian state, how can the rights of the minority, who disagree with the interpretations of the majority, be protected? In short, is there at least a democracy in the Jewish sense of the word, which would protect the rights of the minority?

A: Such protection exists, but only within limits. In the Halacha, rabbis have the right to write, to speak. But all their differences of rulings are based on interpretations of the Halacha itself. If someone speaks against the Halacha, he can of course not be protected. In the Sanhedrin Tractate, the Talmud★ says: at the time of King Hezekiah, the Assyrians attacked Jerusalem and encircled it. So the Assyrians made the Jews an offer: in exchange for their willingness to go into exile, they would be granted a quiet and peaceful life. On the other hand, if they refused to give up, the city would be seized and they would be massacred. So then there was a debate among the Jews in Jerusalem, mainly between the scribe Shebna and the king. The king said: 'God does not want us to surrender to the enemy. It's the Halacha.' And the scribe said: 'We must surrender.' Then it came to a vote. About 130,000 voted in favour of surrender. The king said: 'Maybe we should surrender, since the Bible says that the decision of the majority has to be respected.' Then Isaiah★ came and said to the king: 'It is a vote of wicked people, and the vote of wicked people does not count.' This is the true concept! That of Western democracy is not old enough to be mentioned when discussing the Halacha. As a matter of fact, democracy as we know it today is a totally new concept. It is based on the idea that we are incapable of knowing the truth. And since nobody holds the truth, nobody can say what is true. Therefore the majority has to decide. It's a practical deduction.

Judaism is founded on the idea that we know the truth. So it's absurd to have people vote on the question whether or not we should keep this truth. You don't vote on a truth.

Q: Does that mean that, according to the Halacha, a Jew cannot individually choose his way of life, his life style, and that he has to submit to a collective way of life?

A: A Jewish individual cannot choose a life style contrary to the Halacha. That's the way it is. God created this world for a reason: to have people live in holiness. To talk about free choice, the freedom to be impure, would mean that this world has no reason to exist. With such a freedom there would have been no reason to create this world. This is the essence of our conception of the world and the role of man.

The conception that says that the role of man in Israel is to develop himself, to be happy, to have a guaranteed right to work, etc, can't be the essential purpose of life, but only part of it. The true goal is to be good, to be holy, to make of this world what God wants. Otherwise I don't see what could be the reason for living. At the age of 70 or 80, one dies. Then what?

Let me say it again: democracy and Judaism are two opposite things. One absolutely cannot confuse them. The objective of a democratic state is to allow a person to do exactly as he wishes. The objective of Judaism is to serve God and to make people better. These are two totally opposite conceptions of life.

Q: Yet Judaism is supposed to have given the first example of democracy to humanity. For example, the Jewish people elected King Saul. * So the king was elected, and not imposed on the people.

A: So what? This doesn't prove anything. The first kings all over the world were necessarily chosen by the people. I'm a graduate in political science. I know what I'm talking about. You're right — at the beginning, the first king is elected. Then the people agree to give up some of their rights, for the king to protect them.

The successors of this first king are no longer elected.

But that's not the essential point. The essential point is this: a secular authority can undoubtedly also be chosen through democratic means, but supreme authority must be in the hands of a rabbinic court. It must be wielded by the judges and the rabbis. The Talmud is very clear on this. It says that even if the king wants war, if that war is against the Halacha, the people have the right not to obey their king. One of the problems of secular Judaism, of modern Judaism, is that its ignorance is only surpassed by its arrogance. We live today in a world where ignorant people are arrogant!

When the Jews in Europe were emancipated a century ago, when they came out of their ghettos, they rushed to become French, German or something else, and they immediately forgot that Judaism is completely different to democracy.

Q: Many Jews believe, though, that the objective of Judaism is to deliver a message to the world by living among non-Jews. The reason why there have been so many Jewish scientists, artists, etc is that they have been living among non-Jews.

A: All right. Go ahead. But don't be Jewish. Don't be Jewish! Just be a human being!

Q: Don't you consider that people such as Einstein or Freud were Jewish?

A: They were born Jews. That's all. There's a difference between a Jewish writer and a Jew who is a writer; between a Jewish scientist and a scientist who happens to be Jewish.

Q: Take Freud for example. He wasn't just a psychoanalyst; he was a member of the B'nai B'rith* in Vienna.

A: The fact is, the Jews in Vienna were living in a state of great confusion. The only reason they remained Jewish was because they lived in an anti-Semitic environment. Otherwise they wouldn't have remained Jewish. As a matter of fact, you're just repeating the great insanity of

Zionism. Herzl, this country's big hero, admitted that if the Jews had been given the opportunity to assimilate, they would have accepted assimilation. And it was because the Gentiles wouldn't let us assimilate that Herzl wanted a Jewish state. Now that's not really a very positive reason for founding a state. So we're going to tell our children that if we'd been allowed to assimilate, we would have done so? Is that a good reason for creating a Jewish state? If you say that to a young child or a young person, he's going to tell you: 'If I can get assimilated, I'm going to do it. I'll go to Los Angeles with a US immigration pass, and I'll become an American.'

Q: Would you have preferred that people like Einstein, Freud, Saul Bellow or any other famous Jew... ?

A: I'm not interested in Einstein.

Q: Would you have preferred these people to have been rabbis?

A: By all means. I'd have preferred Einstein to be a rabbi. There are enough people around inventing things in physics. I have nothing against universities: I went to university myself. If someone can be a great scientist within the framework of Judaism, all right, then I agree! But if a Jewish scientist is not a practising Jew, there's no difference between him and any other scientist as far as I am concerned. Oppenheimer is a great scientist. But what do I care? If there's nothing Jewish about him, what's the difference between him and a non-Jew? None. The big swindle of our time is to have twisted Judaism, to have changed it into something that it has never been and that it isn't. God delivered the Jews from slavery in Egypt and gave them a land: the Promised Land. If God's aim had only been to deliver them, and if he hadn't told them to go and build this country, there wouldn't have been this commandment in the Torah ordering us to live in Eretz Yisrael.★ The theory that consists of forgetting this commandment is a theory of fraudulent Jews who don't believe in Judaism and who don't have the courage to say so. And so as to justify themselves, these people say that Judaism is a universal value. But they are wrong. Judaism is not a universal value.

Q: So you don't believe that Judaism could be bipolar?

A: Of course not!

Q: I mean to say that there can be a religious pole and a secular pole and that these two poles could be complementary.

A: Absolutely not! Absolutely not! Of course, a person born a Jew is a Jew. There's no doubt about that. But if he doesn't respect the Torah, he's not a good Jew. The only reason to be Jewish is the Torah. There's no other logical reason to be Jewish. Otherwise he is a Jew by accident, that's all. By accident or for intellectual reasons.

Q: Yet Maimonides,★ the famous Jewish philosopher, lived in Spain among Arabs. He lived in symbiosis with them.

A: That's absolutely false. You're talking nonsense. People who talk about Maimonides like that don't know what they're talking about. The greatness of Maimonides was to have written a book called *The Guide of the Lost.* His greatness came from the fact that he was a rabbi. He codified the Jewish laws. If you had read the laws written by Maimonides, you certainly wouldn't have imagined him to be an enlightened and progressive philosopher. Maimonides was bound by the laws of Judaism. Because that is what Judaism is. I am not free to decide what I want. There is the Halacha; there is a law that decides what is godly and what is not. I live in this country because it is an obligation ordered by God. Otherwise, why would I want to live in a country which, from my point of view, is miserable and uninteresting? If God hadn't ordered us to live in this country, I really wouldn't want to have anything to do with it. Because this country is an absolute disaster, from a geographical as well as a material view-

point. I only live here because it is a holy commandment
to be here. When Maimonides comments on the Halacha,
he speaks about the non-Jews living in Israel, and he says
very clearly that there cannot be Jewish citizenship for a
non-Jew in this country. It's not only Maimonides saying
this. It's God saying it.

*Q: Yet the principal difference between Judaism and Christianity
is that, for a Christian, a supreme authority decides what is right
to do and what not, and that such an authority does not exist for
Jews. Each rabbi interprets the Halacha in his own way, and
there are several legitimate ways of interpreting Judaism.*

A: Nonsense again! To start with, you use the word 'Christianity'. Which Christianity are you talking about? There
are 6,000 Christian sects. And even if you're talking about
the Roman Catholics, you've got some bishops who want
this and others who want that. There's the Pope. But in
France, for example, you've got Father Lefebvre who
opposes the Pope. So don't talk to me about single
authorities in Christianity. True Judaism implies the existence of a Sanhedrin. So there is a supreme authority in
Judaism: the Sanhedrin. I must insist on this: the liberal
Jew commits a terrible fraud, and he commits that fraud
because he would like to be able to decide for himself. In
the same way, a communist Jew does not practise Judaism.
He practises communism. The Jew may be called Cohen,
so then he practises Cohenism! If he's called Goldberg, he
practises Goldbergism! Myself, I practise Judaism. If one
is not bound by the Torah, by the Halacha, then one has
no reason to be a Jew.

Q: When you say that, aren't you talking like Khomeini?

A: OK. Let's say you're right. So what? Who cares? People
who stick labels on you are refusing to talk about the
content. What's the problem? Anyway, I can tell you that
in certain respects Khomeini and Islam are a lot closer to
Judaism than Jean-Jacques Rousseau or John Locke or

Thomas Jefferson. In my mind, there's no doubt about that. If you start from the fundamental concept that it was God who created man, and that one has to obey God's law, then, sure, I'm like Khomeini, or the Pope, or any spiritual leader. I feel much closer to them than to any Rabbi Schindler, who is the leader of liberal Judaism. What this rabbi calls Judaism is just atheism wrapped in a *talith*. ★ Sticking labels on people doesn't lead anywhere. Let's talk about the content.

Q: You have written that the Jews feel guilty about being Jewish, and that they were doing anything they could to please the non-Jews, to get themselves pardoned for being Jewish. Yet in many countries, especially in France, there is a kind of Jewish renaissance. Jews feel proud to be Jewish. Would you call this a new phenomenon?

A: France is a special case. France has three types of Jews. First, the French Jews of old descent, who have always been ashamed of being Jewish. The second category also consists of shamefaced Jews. These are the ones who came from Poland after World War II. Then you have the third category, those who came from North Africa — Morocco and Algeria; this large influx of Jews has brought about a great change in France. I don't know, though, what their children are going to be. There are already many cases of mixed marriages between Jews and non-Jews. The historical perspective must not be viewed in terms of ten or twenty years, but in terms of centuries. Indeed, there are cycles in history, and today one sees a Jewish renaissance in France. But don't forget that today there is also a Jewish state, and that is already a big difference from the past. The big phenomenon, though, is still the mixed marriages, where Jews marry non-Jews while at the same time continuing to say that they are proud to be Jewish; this, to me, is total insanity.

Q: So you make a distinction between being a Jew and being an Israeli.

A: Of course. And that's where the great insanity of this country, the great sickness, comes from. The problem here is not so much the Arabs but the Jews. The secular Jew has a problem of identity. He doesn't know who he is. So he says he is an Israeli. Not a Jew. This is insanity. Because an Arab can also be an Israeli. To be an Israeli means having citizenship of this country. It's not a nationality. So the *sabra*★ lives in a state of complete confusion. He doesn't know who he is. He doesn't know where he's going. People in this country are sick. Intellectually sick. For me, there are no Israelis. There are Jews. Some of them live in Israel. Others live in France. Others live somewhere else. There is a Jewish people. Because there is a Jewish people, we have the right to come to this country, and to take it from the Arabs.

If the *sabra* isn't a Jew, then I don't know why his grand-parents came to this country and took it from the Arabs. It isn't because the Jews lived here 2,000 years ago that they have the right to come back. Who the hell cares whether they lived here 2,000 years ago?

The biggest fascism is precisely that: to believe that one has a right to come back here solely because one lived here 2,000 years ago. The legitimate reason why we have the right to come back here is that we are Jews and because we are Jews we have a 2,000-year bond with this land. We have always prayed three times a day to be able to come back to this land. And we have never given up this hope. It's not the fact that we have come back and that we have created an Israeli state. That's not the reason. The reason is that, first and foremost, we are Jews.

Q: There are supposed to be two traditions. One is Joshua's Judaism, which is a Judaism of conquerors; then there is the Judaism of the prophets, which has a pacifist thread.

A: That's not true at all! Not true at all! These are things that people think when they know absolutely nothing about Judaism. I can quote you the prophets and these quotes will make your hair stand on end. For example, Isaiah spoke of peace, but you should read what he said on the subject of the day when the Messiah will come, and the brutal and bloody way in which he will treat the nations. There are not several messages in Judaism. There is only one. And this message is to do what God wants. Sometimes God wants us to go to war, and sometimes he wants us to live in peace. The Halacha tells us when we should make war and when we should make peace. People who say that there are two messages in Judaism do not actually believe that the Torah was given to us by God. If the Torah was made by men, then it isn't Jewish! There are intelligent people everywhere. Among the Christians, among the Buddhists, among Jews. Among atheists too. But there is only one message: God wanted us to come to this country and to create a Jewish state.

And this Jewish state has been founded so that we can live Jewish values. The Jewish values of peace, among others. The God who addressed Isaiah is the same as the one who spoke to Joshua. The same God gave the same orders to the one and to the other. Just imagine, in Jewish schools in Israel, they teach Joshua according to the Bible! Secular Jews teaching Joshua! If I was a secular Jew, I'd tear out the chapters on Joshua.

Q: For you, does Zionism mean that the Messiah will come soon?

A: Of course, Zionism accelerates the coming of the Messiah. I'm not a nationalist!

Q: What do you mean, you're not a nationalist?

A: I'm not a nationalist. I'm a religious Jew. In Judaism, there is a commandment which says: the Jews are a nation only by the will of God. To be a secular Zionist is absurd. Why should I go to war, fight for one flag rather than another? It's insane. What difference is there between a Finn, a Swede, a Spaniard and a Belgian? For a religious

Jew, nationalism is only one part of Judaism. A part which is under the authority of God.

Q: Do you mean to say that if Zionism is not religious, there is no point in having a state of Israel?

A: For me, the word Zionism means God's order that we live in Israel. And to have this state is a miracle that comes from God. As far as I'm concerned, we are living the end of time. We are living a messianic era. We survived 2,000 years without a state, without an army, without power, scattered to the four corners of the world. Think of the pogroms, of Auschwitz, the concentration camps, the Inquisition — we survived all that! People who believe that we have survived all that, being atheists, are completely blind. The Jews have come back from hundreds of countries just as the Bible said they would. We had a brilliant victory in the Six-Day War, and a few years later, during the Yom Kippur War, we lived through three terrible days. The difference between these two wars is explained by God's will.

If the Jews become religious again and do what God wants, then the Messiah will come today. The creation of the state of Israel only marks the beginning of the messianic era. The Messiah will come. For my part, I don't doubt it for an instant.

The question is, how is he going to come? In the Jewish tradition, he may come in two ways. If we deserve him, he may come at this instant, in glory and in majesty. And if we don't deserve him, he'll come all the same, but in the midst of terrible sufferings. This is why I am fighting today. I am fighting so that the Jews become good Jews, so that there is not a catastrophe at the coming of the Messiah.

Q: When you say that you are not a nationalist, does that mean that the state has no importance?

A: The state is important but it is only as important as any

of the divine commandments, for example the commandment concerning the Sabbath. It is neither more nor less
important. The state is a divine commandment. It is one
means to have a properly Jewish culture. And not to have
a culture influenced by that of the majority. Or by cultures
in which we are in a minority. That's why God has ordered
us to live not in France or in the United States, but in
Israel. Just so as not to be influenced by majority cultures.
God wants us to live in a country of our own, isolated, so
that we live separately and have the least possible contact
with what is foreign, and so that we create as far as possible
a pure Jewish culture based on the Torah. This is why I
am a nationalist, why I want a state: this is what God
wants. And not so as to have a flag like the one you see
outside.

*Q: You have said several times that you want to purify Jewish
culture from any* goy★ *influence.*

A: That's what true Judaism means. I say it very clearly
and very precisely. And all the rabbis say it just as clearly
when you discuss it with them in private. In private they'll
tell you: 'Of course, Kahane is right.' But these rabbis
don't have the courage to say it in public. So what I say
comes as a shock to the Jews.

*Q: Don't terms like purity, purification, bring back bad memories
for Jews... ?*

A: Let me tell you just one thing: does it mean we shouldn't
use tanks, just because the Nazis used tanks? Just because
the Nazis used a certain word doesn't mean that this word
is bad. It depends on how one uses the word. If I say
'money', the word is not in itself satanic. If I use money
to help, I'm making a good action. It makes no sense to
ban a word just because the Nazis used it.

*Q: But the Nazis didn't use the term 'purification' only as a
word. They wanted to 'purify' Germany of any Jewish presence.*

A: Of course! But if the Germans, during World War II, had bombed the Jews, and if the Jews had bombed the Germans, does this mean that Jews and Germans were doing the same thing? No. The Germans had no legitimate reason for wanting to drive the Jews out of Germany. The Germans had stupid, racist ideas. For me, a non-Jew can become a Jew. He has the absolute right to become a Jew. We don't have a blood monopoly. I don't believe in blood. I believe in a culture, an idea. The Germans had no ideal. They based themselves on a concept that was solely racist. To me, a black Jew from Africa is just as Jewish as I am. Last Sunday, I made a speech at Yeruham [a development town] and I attacked the president of the town council because he had refused to admit black Jews to his town. So for me it's not a question of race. It's a matter of ideals. And these ideals are God-given; therefore these ideals have to be propagated here in Israel. Anyone who accepts these ideals is welcome among us.

Q: But it is very difficult to convert to Judaism.

A: Without doubt it is difficult to become a Jew. But it's even more difficult to buy a diamond! It's difficult because we want to be sure that the person who wants to become a Jew does it for sincere reasons... And not just because he's met a pretty Jewish girl and wants to marry her. We have enough bad Jews who were born Jewish; we don't want to add bad converted Jews.

Q: What would you say if all Israeli Arabs decided to convert to Judaism tomorrow?

A: Obviously, we wouldn't agree to it, because they wouldn't want to convert for honest reasons. It takes years to convert a person, don't forget that. Anyway, the Arabs won't do it. They think that Jews are their enemies.

As a matter of fact, leftist Jews despise the Arabs. I don't despise the Arabs. Liberal Jews think that they can buy the Arabs. Jewish racists think that there can be good Arabs, nice Arabs. They believe that they can educate them to be good Arabs. What the leftist Jews call good Arabs are not what I call good Arabs. For me, the good Arab is a proud Arab. And I understand this good Arab. Because I too have national pride.

At the bottom of their hearts, the Israeli Left has this feeling that it is not entirely natural for Jews to be living here in Israel.

So they feel guilty. They feel obliged to defend the Arabs on all the questions they raise, including the end of the Jewish state. But you won't buy the Arabs by raising their standard of living. The Arab is proud and he is concerned about the way his Arab brothers live. And when certain Jews say to the Arabs: 'Look what we've done for you, all the good we have done... We found a desert here and we transformed it into a garden,' the Arab replies, with good reason: 'This may be true, but it was my desert and now it has become your garden.' So I understand the Arabs completely. It's insane to believe that you can buy them, that because you send them to Hebrew university they are going to turn into 'good Arabs' in the sense that the Israeli Left means. It's quite simply false. On the contrary, they will turn into the most dangerous Arabs. Revolutionaries are recruited among the very intellectuals whom we are educating in our universities. We have such a sense of guilt that we keep saying: 'Let's buy them.' You can't buy everything. That's why I say the Arabs must leave Israel, precisely because I believe that if the Arabs stay, they'll become the 'good Arabs' as *I* understand the term.

Q: So that means war, then?

A: No, that doesn't mean war. At the present time, right now, we have the means to show them the door. Twenty years from now, we won't have the power to throw them out.

Q: Why won't you have that possibility twenty years from now?

A: Because in twenty years from now, we'll have as many Arabs as Jews in this country. We have a terrible problem in Israel. It's not the Arabs of the Occupied Territories who are the problem. We can get rid of those Arabs now. The real problem is that there are many Arabs in Israel who have Israeli citizenship. And these Arabs are making many, many children.

Q: Professor Neeman has written that the demographic ratio between Jews and Arabs has not changed since 1967.

A: Another fraud. A statistical fraud. It's a lie by the Tehiya [nationalist party], because this party has a very serious problem: it wants to annex the Occupied Territories and keep the Arabs living there. The real question is the following: do we need another million and a half Arabs? In fact, the latest statistics show that Arabs from the West Bank territories go to work in Kuwait because there's work there and there's no work here. Besides, Neeman is talking about the Arabs living in the Territories, but I'm talking about the Arabs who have Israeli citizenship. And this Arab population is growing twice as fast as the Jewish population. Israel's Arabs are high-quality Arabs; they all go to school, they are intelligent; they have tremendous qualities. Northern Israel will be completely Arab in the near future. Galilee already has an Arab majority. Umm el-Fahm [a village in Galilee] already has an overwhelming Arab majority.

We're sitting here doing nothing, watching what is happening without lifting a finger. Once the Arabs have a majority in this country, they're going to do what any self-respecting nationalist would do. They are not going to accept living in a country called a Jewish state, in a country with a Law of Return that applies solely to the Jews. Once the Arabs have gained a majority, they'll change the laws and the nature of this state, and they'll be right. Completely right. And this is why I want to move them all out now. I say now, because we need a minimum of force to do it.

If I were the minister of defence, if I were talking to you now as minister of defence, the mere fact of hearing me say what I just said would sow panic among the Arabs. The Arabs are afraid of me, because they know that I understand them.

Q: Are you intending to drive the Arabs out by military means?

A: Yes, obviously, but that won't be necessary for most of them. I'd offer financial compensation for those who want to leave the country voluntarily. I would only use force for those who don't want to leave. I'd go all the way, and they know that.

Q: Do you have the money to offer them that kind of compensation?

A: That money could come, from Jews all over the world.

Q: Do you really believe that the Jews would pay?

A: Of course, because the Arabs have property, and that property would remain behind.

Q: If an Arab came to you right now and said: 'OK, give me some money to leave,' would you give it to him?

A: No. I don't have any money, and it's not my job to make such payments. It's the job of the Israeli government, of the Jewish people, to give the money. It's not mine.

I'd like to raise another question here: the Arabs owe a lot of money to the Sephardic Jews who were obliged to leave Arab countries without compensation. I want an account of everything the Jews from Arab countries left behind them. Then we'll see who owes money to whom.

In any case, I am prepared to offer compensation, and the amount of the compensation will depend on what the Jews from the Arab countries left behind. But in any event, we're going to have to offer the Arabs something so as to stimulate them to leave.

The real problem is that I am not about to ask them to leave. I want to make them leave. I'm saying to them that they must leave, and I'll make them leave. As to the circumstances under which they are going to leave, this is not up to them to decide.

Q: Therefore it won't be your party that will expel the Arabs. What you want is to force the government to do it.

A: Of course! Because there are no other practical means of doing it. You need government means for an action like this. But I'm convinced that my party will be in the government. I have no doubt about that.

Q: In the meantime, you engage in actions such as in Umm el-Fahm or in Taibeh, to scare the Arabs and to force them to leave.

A: Absolutely. I want to scare them and I want to make them realize that, contrary to what they have believed for fifteen years, time is not on their side. That it is completely false that time is on their side. They are convinced that it is the Jews who are afraid. But I, I go to see them in Umm el-Fahm, and I tell them: 'You must leave now.' And that changes everything.

I'm smart enough not to use force. Because that's just what the police would like to see me do. I believe that within five years, we're going to be part of a coalition government, at least.

Q: Your party, the Kach, has been accused of having close links with the Jewish terrorist group TNT. You are believed to have planned attacks on mosques and other similar actions.

A: I don't like to talk about these accusations. When someone calls me a Nazi, I don't answer him. I'm not obliged to answer every dog that barks. If you come to see me with proof that I have committed such acts, then I'll discuss it with you. This doesn't mean that I believe that such actions shouldn't have been committed. But I think that such actions are not opportune for the moment. Because we're soon going to be in the government. That's why people on the Left are afraid of us.

They believe that I have no political future in Israel, but they're still obsessed by me.

Q: Still, one of the members of your party, Richter, is in prison because of terrorist activities. You do admit, don't you, that Richter has committed acts of violence?

A: Yes, of course he has.

Q: And he is a member of your party?

A: Obviously, I completely agree with Richter. But he didn't commit these acts as a member of the Kach party. He committed them on behalf of himself, as a person called Richter. Besides, I can assure you that if the police had the slightest evidence against the Kach, I wouldn't be sitting here talking to you now. I'd be in prison. Believe me, Kach won't give them this satisfaction.

Q: Does that mean that Kach does not encourage violence, but if a member of Kach commits acts of violence, you support him?

A: This applies not only to Kach members, but to anybody. And I approve of anybody who commits such acts of violence. Really, I don't think that we can sit back and watch Arabs throwing rocks at buses whenever they feel like it. They must understand that a bomb thrown at a Jewish bus is going to mean a bomb thrown at an Arab bus.

Q: One of your paradoxes is that you respect the Arabs and their nationalism, yet you want to expel them for precisely that reason. You also say that no Arab is innocent. Isn't that a racist comment?

A: Of course no Arab is innocent.

Q: What do you mean by that?

A: That every Arab is a proud Arab, a good nationalist. And because of this, he is opposed to the existence of the state of Israel. When the Allies, during World War II, bombed German towns, who did they kill? Women, children... They could only do such a thing because it was a war against the German people. When the Maquis in

France took action against the Germans, they didn't care whether they killed military or civilian Germans — it was war.

War is war. Either you fight or you don't fight. The 'Palestinians', as they call themselves, are enemies of the state of Israel. Obviously, not every Palestinian is a bomb-thrower. Not all Frenchmen threw bombs at the Germans during World War II. Not everybody had the courage to do it, nor to join the underground resistance movements. In the same way, there are Arabs who have the courage to throw bombs, and others who don't.

Q: So you accept the fact that Arab civilians are being killed?

A: Of course. Sure. In the same way that I wholly approved of the Israelis bombing Lebanon. Unfortunately, many civilians were killed. But this is war...

Q: You've said in the Knesset, and it was shown on Israeli television, that if you were in power no Arab would be killed because you wouldn't let any Arabs stay here.

A: I don't want to kill any Arab. I want to move them out. I want them to live happily in peace, but not here in Israel. Somewhere else!

Q: But that's a jihad, *a holy war, that you want to conduct against the Arabs.*

A: No, it's not a *jihad* on my side. It's a *jihad* on *their* side.

Q: What do you want to do with the Christians in Israel? Do you want to throw them out too?

A: Any non-Jew, including the Arabs, can have the status of a foreign resident in Israel if he accepts the law of the Halacha. I don't differentiate between Arabs and non-Arabs. The only difference I make is between Jews and non-Jews. If a non-Jew wants to live here, he must agree to be a foreign resident, be he Arab or not. He does not have and cannot have national rights in Israel. He can have civil rights, social rights, but he cannot be a citizen; he won't have the right to vote. Again, whether he's Arab or not.

Q: So you would accept having Arabs in Israel, as foreigners.

A: Certainly. But since I know and respect them, I know very well that no Arab under the age of 40 would accept such a situation. Just as the Blacks in South Africa won't accept a similar situation. But there is a big difference over there, because South Africa belongs to the Blacks.

Q: Let me ask you again: what would you do if the Arabs opted for the status of foreign residency?

A: I don't think that they would accept it. Some of them, maybe, but only a few.

Q: You said just now that in twenty years, Israel will no longer have the strength to expel the Arabs. Why are you so worried about the future, given that the state of Israel has won every war since Israel was created?

A: I'm not talking about a war; I'm talking about *inside* the country. These are two different problems. In twenty years, the Arabs *inside the country* will be 35-40 per cent of the population. They will all be citizens. There isn't a country in the world which has two peoples in it, which has such a demographic distribution, and which has been able to live in peace. Look what's happening even in those countries where the differences between the two communities are not so great, where, for example, there is only a simple religious difference between Catholic and Protestant Christians. Here we are different from the Arabs in every way. We speak a different language, we have different religions! There's bound to be a bloody civil war here between those two population groups, and once the Arabs make up 40 per cent of the population, it's going to be a terrible problem.

Q: You want to throw them out — but where to? If nobody

wants to take them, what are you going to do with them? It is very likely that no Arab state is going to accept them.

A: I'm not asking anybody to accept them. I'm going to hold the bridges on the Jordan river; we'll hold them for two weeks. We'll evacuate the Arabs and let Jordan go to the United Nations. What I am concerned about is the survival of the state of Israel as a Jewish state, and I can't sit and worry about whether this or that is going to happen.

Q: You once said that if no solution can be found, you'd put them into work camps.

A: I've never said that. They are going to have to get out of here. That's all.

Q: After the massacres of Sabra and Chatila, you wrote that it should have been the Israelis who did it.

A: I said that this was what Israel should have done, not after seizing the camps, but during the actual fighting. The Israeli government was responsible for the deaths of sixty to seventy Israeli soldiers. It is responsible because it sent them inside PLO areas, PLO nests, without the backing of air support, without anything. Not even artillery. It was insanity to send them like that, under the pretext that the civilian population should not be harmed. Plain murder! This is why I said that these 'civilian' camps should have been bombed in the first place. Of course, once these camps had been bombed, one should not have killed the survivors.

Q: According to you, where are the exact borders of Eretz Yisrael?

A: The borders that are mentioned in the Bible.

Q: But there are different interpretations among the rabbis...

A: Let me tell you what the minimal borders are, and which the rabbis agree upon, according to the description given in the Bible. The southern boundary goes up to El Arish, which takes in all of northern Sinai, including Yamit. To the east, the frontier runs along the western part of the

East Bank of the Jordan river, hence part of what is now Jordan. Eretz Yisrael also includes part of the Lebanon and certain parts of Syria, and part of Iraq, all the way to the Tigris river.

Q: But that would mean perpetual war with the Arabs.

A: There will be a perpetual war. With or without Kahane. It's not Kahane who wants it. It's because the Arabs believe that the Jews are thieves. I can understand the Arabs' point of view. It has nothing to do with what the boundaries are. Whether they're here or there makes no difference. When Israel accepted the 1947 boundary, the Arabs said no. Then the Arabs would not accept the 1949 boundary, and then the 1967 boundary. The Arabs won't accept *any* boundary. The Arabs believe that this country belongs to them, and I can understand them. Therefore there *will* always be war. It's not so terrible. It's nothing exceptional. I've served in the army. My son serves in the army. And my son–in–law serves in the army.

Q: So, in your opinion, according to Judaism, violence is legitimate?

A: Everything has its place. The Bible says that there is a time for war and a time for peace. Sometimes the Bible commands Jews to go to war. Sometimes it commands them to live in peace. When you are in danger, then it is an obligation to go to war; you have to go to war. If you are not in danger, then you should not go to war.

Q: As far as your party is concerned, you have said that violence would be political suicide without the support of public opinion in Israel.

A: Absolutely. That's true. That's why I tell my people not to use violence. Not for any moral reason, but because it would be stupid to recommend violence. Because once the police arrest them, they will not get the backing of public opinion. You have to know when is the right time to use violence. Right now, we have a political opportunity to win ten seats in the Knesset. And at the next elections it is certain that we will be the third largest party in Israel. Then we'll be a government party.

Q: Is violence between and among Jews legitimate?

A: It depends on the circumstances. For example, if we began a programme to move the Arabs out, and there were Jews who opposed this programme, even though it was a government law, then we would have to use force against them. That's sad. But they would have to obey.

Q: What would happen if the present government decided to give back all or part of the West Bank? Would you oppose it by force?

A: No. Not by physical force. We would use civil disobedience. We would put up passive resistance, just as we did in Yamit. There's no question that there's a real possibility that this may happen and that the Labour Party is ready to do it. I'm convinced that very many Jews would fight that, but, again, not necessarily by resorting to force. But the government will not be in a position to evacuate these places if 50,000 Jews barricade themselves in their houses. Peres will not risk a civil war in the country.

Q: If you say that the realization of Eretz Yisrael is a divine objective, isn't that the same as saying that this objective lies beyond existing laws?

A: Absolutely! Absolutely! But I know that if we used force against the army, we would lose. No religious commandment orders us to commit suicide in order to have Jewish law. But there can be no doubt whatsoever: according to Jewish law, we have the duty, even the obligation, to use force in order to prevent any government violating the laws of Judaism. Therefore I'll wait until I'm in command.

Q: Many people in Israel believe that your politics and your programme are a provocation and that they help the Left in Israel and the Arabs to form an anti-Israeli front. What do you think about that?

A: The Tehiya also think that, although they too are fighting for the realization of Eretz Yisrael. They are worried that we will take two seats from them in the next elections! That is of course true. They can't fight us on an ideological or political level; they can't find any good arguments against us. Because their plan to annex the Territories and the Arabs living there is absurd. Anyway, to answer your question, the non-Zionists have always said that Zionism is a provocation against the Arabs. Obviously it is a provocation. So what? Any nationalism is a provocation to other nationalisms.

Q: Do you expect to come to power through elections alone?

A: Yes... But if you ask me what is going to happen in this country in the near future, I'd answer that things aren't that simple. The economic problems are so very serious; the government is a fraud, just like every other government. Democracy breeds governments that are fraudulent, because a government which has to rely on its voters for its existence cannot tell the truth. The bitter truth. If they say: 'We have to cut down on this... we must reduce that...' people won't vote for them. Therefore the government has to lie. That's what democracy is all about! Democracy is like a compost, it nurtures fraud and lies. And it must lead to a dictatorship eventually. Because since a democratic government doesn't have the courage to take the steps that are needed, problems are bound to get worse, and in the end the people will accept dictatorship. This train of events may happen here, precisely because the majority of people in this country have no experience of democracy. Even without Kahane, democracy means nothing to them. Therefore we might get a dictatorship here, if the unemployment situation gets worse.

Q: In your opinion, who would be the best candidate as a dictator?

A: At this moment, Sharon, without any doubt. He has the best claim. But he is a very, very bad person.

Q: Why?

A: He is very bad! I'm not talking about his political views. I don't judge him according to his views. He's bad. He's a liar. He has no moral principles. He has no ideals. He's capable of doing anything, and I'm just as afraid of him as the Left are.

Q: Then you wouldn't approve of a dictatorship under Sharon?

A: Absolutely not.

Q: Most of your militants are Americans. How do you explain this?

A: That's not true. Obviously, the 27,000 people who voted for me are not Americans. It's just another lie they're spreading about me. I must say that as an immigrant from the United States, I'm not used to the kind of lies they tell in Israel. I'm not used to the corruption, the perversion of truth. Because, in this country, the truth is perverted. Sure, there are Americans in my movement, like there are in all the political parties. But we also have a high percentage of the new Russian immigrants among us. Because these new immigrants see in us a real Zionist movement. We proclaim the centrality of Judaism in this country.

Q: What is your social and economic programme?

A: I don't know what a 'social programme' means in this world. In terms of economic programme, there is no doubt that this country needs to put an end to the clawing fingers of all the bureaucrats. This country has to encourage private enterprise. We need capital. Israel has a unique chance which you find in no other country. An unbelievable number of Jews of the Diaspora are prepared to help this country and are already helping it. But nobody is prepared to come to Israel to set up a business when he has to crawl at the feet of government officials to get support. Government officials in this country can drive you crazy.

Economic power is the basis of political power. And the establishment, the institutions of Right and Left, all these people who have political power, are not ready to allow the development of free enterprise here. Yet they need private capital. But they want to get it on their own terms. We should do everything to stimulate private investments. We must give incentives to people who want to invest, to build factories here. Factories create new jobs. They create export potential, which will provide the foreign currency which we so badly need. We must pass laws that release private enterprise from the claws of the Israeli bureaucracy.

Q: So far as economics are concerned, then, you're a liberal?

A: Yes. That's my first answer to the question. My second answer is as follows: 98 per cent of the land in this country belongs to the government. Why? The land should be given to young couples so that they can build on it. Keeping land in the hands of the government is typical of the mentality of Eastern Europe.

But I also believe that the state has social obligations. For example, there has to be a minimum wage; this is not enforced here. It's a disgrace to have young Arabs at the age of 13 or 14 working in Jewish factories. A disgrace! There must be social laws. Judaism is based upon social conscience, on goodness, on generosity. A Jewish state must not have one set of social laws for Jews and another for non-Jews. They must be the same for everybody. Most important, though, this country must be opened up to private investment by the Jews of the Diaspora. Then we would have a tremendous country. And a flourishing one.

This country was created by Jews coming from the dictatorships of Eastern Europe, who had no background whatsoever in concepts of being liberal. In their own way, they were Bolsheviks. This must change.

When these Jews arrived here, they believed that this country was theirs, it was their property. They make me laugh when they talk to me about democracy. How did they treat the Sephardic Jews? When the Sephardis arrived in 1948, they put them into transit camps. And any Sephardic Jew looking for a job had to show his Histadrut* card first. Without this card, he didn't get the job. Would you call it democratic to put young Yemeni Jews into leftist *kibbutzim*,* forcing them not to respect the Sabbath?

These East European Jews have an anti-democratic background. They are the ones who kidnapped members of the Irgun and Stern and turned them over to the British occupation forces; they were the ones who fired on the *Altalena*,* killing nineteen Jews. Rabin was the commander of the operation. So let them not talk to me about their moral principles and their love for the Jews!

Q: Today's young Israelis are far more attracted by material comforts than by Zionist ideals. Doesn't this mental attitude work against the establishment of settlements in Judea and Samaria? Is there sufficient pioneer spirit to colonize the West Bank?

A: Were there enough people in the 1920s who wanted to come to Israel? Today, if we had a government which was really committed to creating settlements, we wouldn't have this problem. We don't have to reproduce the same material conditions as in 1920! We can set up settlements that are more comfortable. If they were given free housing, many young people and young couples would come. The issue you are raising, though, is far more complex and more serious. Western democracy feeds everything that is wrong and sick in human nature. The parties compete with each other in promising people an easy life. The main concept of democracy is that people should believe that they need to have more. There, the only true value is that of wanting more. But that's exactly what's happening here. Everyone says that the Sephardic Jews who came to settle in Israel were backward people! Yet these Jews arrived here with very deep values. And these values were taken away from them and replaced by Dizengoff Street values [Tel Aviv's Oxford Street]. By materialism! It's really unbelievable! Insane! It's a sickness! You listen to people talking on a bus. What are they talking about? All they can talk about is money. That's what this country has made of them. This is not a Jewish state. It's a Hebrew-speaking Portugal that would like to be a Hebrew-speaking Sweden or America. This is our tragedy! And it has to change. Our struggle is not a political struggle; it is an ideological struggle, a struggle of two different concepts of life, two different concepts of the world. We want to create this country with Jewish values. As I have said many times in the Knesset, it is a struggle between the 'Hellenists'* of our time and the Jews who want to remain Jewish.

Q: In other words, you want to revert to the ideals of the founding fathers of Israel, to the pioneer values of Zionism.

A: No! The founding fathers created this state of affairs without realizing what they were doing. When you take Judaism away from Zionism, when you create a secular Zionism, you create this state of affairs. Secular Zionism — what is that supposed to mean? Why should someone live in a *kibbutz*? Why? Tell me! If he is taught that the main thing in life is to live better, to have a more comfortable life... for me, life in a *kibbutz* is not happiness!

The only basic values in life are those which are commanded by God. The others are temporary. They may be good for you, but not for me. Certain values may be good for one time but not for another. That's why the idealistic *kibbutz* concept of the founding fathers has failed. The *kibbutzim* have failed. They mean nothing to young people.

Q: Does this mean that you are in favour of a patriarchal state?

A: It means that there must be a state governed by the Torah. Schools must be impregnated by the Torah and the teachings of the rabbis. Maybe I'm going too far: I don't

know to what extent the Sephardic Jews who are supporting me now on the Arab question will support me in other
matters.

*Q: You once said that you were more afraid of the Jews than of
the Arabs.*

A: Yes, that's true. I know the Arabs. I know how to deal
with them. But I can't throw the Jews out of the country.
I can't do that to them! So the problem is not simple.

*Q: What do you think about the other Israeli parties who try to
limit your freedom of action and to marginalize you? There seems
to be an anti-Kahane unanimity in the Israeli establishment,
ranging from the Left to the Right.*

A: As I said before, I raise a terribly painful problem for
the Left, when I say that Zionism is completely incompatible with Western democracy, and when I ask: Why be a
Jew? Why have a Jewish state? I bother them much more
than the communists do. When I raise the issue of a fundamental Jewish state, they realize that it is a basic issue. The
Right, to a large extent, has the same problem. The Right
also has no logical reason to be Jewish. Plus, of course, I
am taking votes from them. That's what bothers them
most of all. Likud realizes that I'll take many seats away
from them. I'm going to take two seats from the Tehiya
too. Therefore they'd rather see me disappear.

*Q: But even some Israelis who have taken action against the
Arabs and who should be sympathizing with you have declared
from their prison cells that they have nothing in common with you.*

A: Obviously. If people knew that they have links with
Kach, they would get a much tougher sentence. I know
them very well. I visit them in prison. In private, they
most certainly don't think what you've just been saying.

*Q: Likud doesn't seem to have a clearly defined attitude towards
you. Shamir, for example, disapproves of your activities, yet he
wasn't present at the vote to restrict your parliamentary immunity.*

A: That's true. The Likud people are confused. Contrary to them, we have an ideological concept. As a matter of fact, they're afraid. Because they know that they'd lose even more votes if they voted to get me out of the Knesset.

In fact they don't know what to do with me. Take that vote restricting my immunity! That was a mistake! When they passed that bill, they doubled the number of my followers.

Q: What kind of relationship do you have with the people of Gush Emunim?

A: A good relationship. We are on excellent terms with Rabbi Levinger. But they are a single-issue movement: the land, the land of Israel. That's fine. But this country has other problems besides the establishment of settlements: social problems, problems with the Arabs, religious problems. And our party deals with all these problems.

Q: Have members of Kach established settlements in Judea and Samaria?

A: No. The government will not allow us. We have tried to settle there for years, but in vain.

Two years ago, we tried to seize a part of this territory. We settled on a hill. The government was convinced that we wouldn't be able to hold out through the winter. But we did. Then the army came and forced us out.

Q: How many members are there in the Kach party?

A: Maybe 5-6,000. People here don't join parties. They vote for a party. Not like in France or the United States. Here, the real power is determined by the number of votes given during elections, by the number of seats in the Knesset. What is important here is knowing whether you are able to take power, to enter the government.

Q: Economically, and to a large extent militarily, Israel depends on the United States. Do you believe that the United States will allow you to apply your programme concerning the Arabs?

A: I don't have to ask the Americans' approval. The United States, just like any other country in the world, is not ruled by ideals. De Gaulle once said: 'There are no allies, there are only interests.' If the United States believes that Israel is in line with its interests, then there's nothing Israel can't do. But if the United States thinks differently, then there's nothing that Israel can do which will have American backing. It's simply a matter of interests. At the end of World War II, the American government backed Franco. It supported Salazar. It supports Pinochet. Just as France will support any country that buys jet planes from it. And so on. China is now giving its support to such 'peaceloving' countries as Pakistan.

Your question contains a much deeper and more important aspect, though. Whatever happens to Israel will happen by God's will. I believe in God. Most people, even practising Jews, don't believe in God. They play a game. They pray to God but they don't really believe in the existence of God. I, however, I believe that God really exists, and that God decides what is going to happen. And he decides on the basis of whether we deserve it. The essential concept of Judaism is faith that God is stronger, stronger than any government. Yet this country is governed by people who don't believe in anything, who have no faith. Therefore they are terrified by the Americans. Shultz writes an absolutely disgraceful letter to Peres, telling him to straighten up economic matters in his country. And Peres obeys. We have become a people of beggars who don't believe in themselves, and certainly don't believe in God. If the Jews believed in God, God would arrange for America to back Israel. Even Ronald Reagan can't do as he wishes. He is an instrument in the hands of God. And in the end, he is going to do what God wants him to do. That's how a devout Jew should be talking.

If we go on like this, without Kahane — forget Kahane — this country will become a vassal of the United States.

And it will give up the West Bank. It will do so if America says: 'Do it; otherwise you won't get any more money.'

God repays blow for blow, measure for measure. Now we are being punished. We do not trust in God. We looked to Washington. Now we have to pay the price. If I was prime minister, I'd talk to Washington exactly as I'm talking to you. I'd say: 'Stop bothering me. Next time you want to find out how your F16 performs in combat, I'll tell you to find somebody else to tell you; and if you want a captured Soviet T72 tank from us, I'll tell you to find someone else to capture one.' That's how I would talk to the Americans. And after that, I'd go to the synagogue to pray.

Q: In 1968, you created the Jewish Defense League in the United States, to defend the poor Jews against the Blacks.

A: No. Not necessarily against the Blacks. Against anybody who attacked them. The ones who were attacking them happened to be black, but I'd have done the same thing if they had been blond Swedes.

Q: Didn't you create this League because you had special problems with the Blacks in the United States?

A: I have problems neither with the Blacks, nor with the Whites, nor with the Yellows, nor with the Greens. I have problems only with anti–Semites.

Q: Do you think that your actions abroad against the Soviet Union produced results?

A: There's not the slightest doubt. The exodus of Jews from the USSR started in 1968-69 because the problems of these Jews were making headline news thanks to our actions. Before that, nobody knew that such a dramatic problem existed.

We wanted to threaten the *détente* between the United States and the USSR. The Russians, of course, weren't afraid of the Jewish Defense League. But the actions of the

League threatened *détente*, and that is what the Russians were afraid of.

The USSR is not Luxemburg, don't forget that. When the ambassador of Luxemburg is beaten up in the streets, it's not very serious. But if the first secretary of the Soviet Embassy is beaten up in the streets of New York, it is a humiliation to a superpower, and they then recall their ambassador.

The USSR had to react. But how could it react best? What did it need most of all? Science, technology, foreign currency, wheat, or keeping the Jews? For the USSR, it was better to let the Jews go. That's exactly what happened.

Q: But emigration of Russian Jews has come to an end.

A: It came to an end because the Jewish Defense League stopped its actions.

Q: Does the League no longer exist?

A: It still exists, but it hasn't done much during the past seven or eight years. It is no longer what it used to be. Therefore, obviously, you could say that the actions of the League have influenced the position of Jews emigrating from the USSR.

I'll say it again: thanks to the League, the problem made the headlines. If you want to solve a problem, you must first let people know that it exists. This was the first step. The second step was to give the Jews inside the USSR an enormous amount of support. They finally became aware of the fact that other Jews, outside of the USSR, cared about them. The worst thing for a prisoner is not knowing whether anybody cares about him. The third step was to push the other Jewish organizations into doing things. The so-called extremists are the ones who push moderate people into doing things that they would never have done otherwise.

Q: Have you given up the League now?

A: No. But now I live in Israel, and it is very difficult to lead an organization that is located in the United States. Any activist group must have a very strong leader. People who come into this kind of organization are violent people. They must be strictly kept in hand. You have to know how to calm them down. And it is not easy to find people in the United States who are capable of filling this role. Leaders don't grow on trees. Officially, I'm still the head of the League. But in practical terms it is difficult for me to run it from here.

Q: But aren't you sharing your time between Israel and the United States?

A: Yes. Out of every five weeks, I spend one week in the United States. But to run the League, I would have to be in the States full-time. Otherwise it's not going to work.

Q: The League was created to defend the Jews of the Diaspora. But why do they need to be defended when they have succeeded so well everywhere, except perhaps in the USSR?

A: If you had analysed the situation of the Jews during the 1920s, you would have come to the same conclusion. From 1820 to 1920, you could have demonstrated by a graph that the situation of the Jews was constantly improving. Liberalism was in the ascendant.

Fraternity too. If, in 1925, somebody had said: 'In twenty years from now, one third of European Jews will have been massacred,' he would have been called insane. The reason why the situation of the Diaspora is good today is because the world economic situation seems to be good. In reality, the world is heading for an economic collapse of monumental proportions. Western Europe is already beginning to suffer today, and tomorrow it's going to have the same problems as Israel. Nobody can spend more money than he makes. If you're an individual, the bank will stop giving you loans within a day. A city can go on a little longer, but in the end it will collapse. Then we are going to be faced with a terrible wave of anti-Semitism. Worse than in Germany.

Why? Because the West is like a drug addict. The West is addicted to materialism. A person in the Western world who loses his house or his car turns into an animal. And since everybody believes that all Jews are Rothschilds, that they are obviously and even ostentatiously rich, so Jews are going to be the main target of people's hatred. Anybody can detect anti-Semitism when it is already there. But not everybody has the ability to foresee anti-Semitism to-morrow. The Talmud says: 'The wise man can foresee the future.' Therefore we have to be wise.

I'll add this: according to Judaism, according to the rab-bis, God does not want Jews to live in foreign countries. He wants them to go home. And if they refuse to go home, they risk having to pay for it with a great tragedy.

This state of Israel came into being not because Jews wanted it, but because they had no other choice. Without the holocaust, there wouldn't have been a state of Israel. The overwhelming majority of Jews came into this country because they had no choice. As soon as a Jew has a choice, he doesn't come here. Or, what's even worse, he leaves here. Jews here have forgotten that they had no other choice.

Q: You have an apocalyptic view of the Jews' destiny.

A: Yes, of course, for the time being. But in the end, I have a beautiful vision, because then the Messiah will come.

Q: Have you been working to set up a concrete and effective organization for the Jews of the Diaspora to defend themselves?

A: Yes.

Q: You have been accused, for example, of having smuggled weapons all round the world in order to arm the Jews.

A: Yes, I've done that.

Q: Why?

A: Because I can't say to the Jews: 'If you don't want to go to Israel, so much the worse for you, there's nothing I can do for you.' I can't do that.

I have to tell them: 'Jews, get out!' That's the only thing I have to tell them. However, I also say: 'If you can't leave, I have an obligation to help you; and perhaps then, in the meantime, you will realize that emigrating to Israel is the only right thing to do.'

So, in any event, I have to warn the Jews of the potential danger. I can't just sit back and say to myself: 'If they don't want to listen to me, I won't help them.'

This is why I created the Jewish Defense League, and our motto 'Never Again' does not mean that 'it' will never happen again. That would be nonsense. It means that if it happens again, it won't happen in the same way. Last time, the Jews behaved like sheep.

Q: Are you still helping the Jews of the Diaspora to get organized?

A: Absolutely, yes. That's the reason, by the way, why I'm barred from Canada, Belgium and England. Someone is trying to organize a trip to France for me. Up to now I've not been barred from France...

Q: It won't take long, though!

A: ...It's a pity, because in Canada, we have a very strong section of the JDL, surprisingly. There's another one in England. There was also one in France, but now several other Jewish self-defence groups have been set up there, which are excellent.

Q: You must be talking of the Betar...

A: No, I'm talking about the organization headed by a lawyer...

Q: Hadjenberg?

A: Yes.

Q: Where do you get your money from?

A: We get very substantial support from the American Jews. Many rich Jews give me a lot of money, but they won't admit it openly.

Q: I believe you once had links with the Mafia...

A: That's absolutely right.

Q: With Colombo?

A: Yes, with Colombo. But you couldn't really call it 'links'.

Q: What was the connection, then?

A: At that time, Colombo was faced with several law suits. Most members of the Mafia have never realized how important public relations are. But he did. And that's the reason why he was killed.

Colombo had decided to create a civil rights movement for Americans of Italian descent. He needed to establish contacts with other ethnic groups, not just Jews, but others too. He didn't know much about the Jews. So he asked around who was the most popular rabbi in America. Somebody told him about Kahane. Not that I was exactly popular... At that time, many rabbis were already against me. Colombo turned up in the following manner: thirteen of our people were being brought up for trial and we needed bail money. He gave us the necessary money. He did it for a very simple reason: to win sympathy among the Jews. His group took part in demonstrations for the Jews in the Soviet Union. He was on American television, saying that the Italian Americans backed the rights of Jews in the USSR. As for us, we never did anything for him, apart from the fact that by helping us, he strengthened his own cause.

I'd take help from anybody. If the state of Israel took help from Joseph Stalin, then I could take help from Joe Colombo. That's all there is to my relationship with the Mafia. You can't really call it 'links'.

Q: But did you help each other in illicit arms deals?

A: We certainly did.

Q: Didn't you have another name before 1965?

A: Yes, I was called Michael King.

Q: Did you work for the FBI then?

A: Yes, I worked for the FBI.

Q: What can you tell us about that period?

A: Together with a friend of mine, I worked in a small research group in Washington. At that time, the FBI wanted to get more information about the actions of the right-wing, not just the left-wing, movements. The FBI came to see us, knowing that we were Jewish, and offered us a contract. Our work consisted of infiltrating the John Birch Society, and I was very keen on doing it, because it was an extreme-Right, anti-Semitic and very dangerous movement. I infiltrated them over a period of three years. I had a new name, a new address, etc...

Q: So you were an underground FBI agent in the Birch Society?

A: I became a member of the organization and was able to discover the source of their funding. It was a great service rendered to the Jewish cause. Since 1965-66, the John Birch Society has been reduced to nothing.

Q: Are you going to write a book about this experience?

A: I'm not going to write any kind of biography; all biographies are the height of egoism. Whenever I have some time, I sit and study the Torah. If I had the time to write, I'd write about the Torah. Not about myself.

Q: So you infiltrated the John Birch Society. But we've heard that you also infiltrated left-wing movements.

A: That's not true.

Q: You helped the FBI against student movements opposing the Vietnam War...

A: That's not right. Granted, I was a strong defender of the Vietnam War. But I did not work for the FBI in this connection.

At that time I believed, and I still believe it, that a weak America is a bad thing for Israel. The only power that protects the free world from the Soviet Union is America. In my opinion, no other superpower of the size of America has done as good a job as America. It has the means to conquer, to take over the world, but it hasn't.

The problem with the Vietnam War was not whether it was a good or a bad war. The problem was that a defeat for the United States would have given rise to a hostile movement in the United States against sending troops to any other part of the world. Unfortunately that's what happened, and now we feel the consequences of this reaction. I never fought against leftist movements. All these rumours are absurd.

Many of the things that were written about me at that time aren't true.

Q: Do you mind if I ask you a personal question? You have been a rabbi, and you were dismissed...

A: Unlike France, America does not have a consistory that deals with this problem centrally. In America, you have total anarchy: a few people can get together and decide to create a synagogue. And they create synagogues not so much for religious reasons, but more for social, almost mundane reasons. All right, some Jews created a synagogue. They needed a rabbi. They hired me for the ceremonies, weddings, funerals, etc... I had a lot of influence on the children; they liked me. Because of me, the children started to practise the religion, to observe the Sabbath. This really upset the parents. The children started eating kosher food, but their parents' homes were not kosher. Therefore I was dismissed from the synagogue. The people still liked me. They said to me: 'Rabbi, please stay! Just stop converting our children!' I couldn't accept that condition, and resigned.

Anyway, I no longer wanted to be a rabbi. It's not the right job for a good Jewish boy.

Q: But to be a lawyer is a good job for a good Jewish boy. Why didn't you practise law, then?

A: I studied law because I wanted to serve in the Foreign Ministry here. That's why I did my degree in international law. But I couldn't join the Foreign Ministry because I wasn't a member of the Labour Party...

Anyway, I never dreamed that I would be doing what I'm doing now. I didn't have the least idea.

Q: Didn't you plan your political career?

A: No. When I was in the United States, I was the editor of the *Jewish Press*; that's where the idea came to me to create the Jewish Defense League. As editor of the *Jewish Press*, I heard about many things that were not printed in the newspapers. That's when I decided to create the League.

Q: Why did you wait until 1971 before settling in Israel?

A: I did not wait! As a matter of fact, I had planned to go to Israel as soon as I was done with my FBI job, in 1966. But I didn't have the money. I had to go to work to make money. I had to put it off. Then, in 1968, I created the Jewish Defense League.

They told me that the League would collapse if I left then. Which was true, by the way. Another three years went by. By that time I had children and I was afraid they would speak Hebrew with an accent. So then I decided to leave. For the League, it was a big mistake. But for me, the time had come to go to Israel.

Q: Why do you keep your American passport?

A: For obvious reasons. I can't go to Canada as it is. And if I no longer had my American passport, I wouldn't be able to go to the United States either. That's the only reason.

Q: Besides religion and politics, do you have any hobbies? You like baseball, don't you?

A: I love baseball. I'm a great sports fan, but I no longer have time for things like that. When I have time, my greatest pleasure is to sit down and study the Torah. It is an extraordinary intellectual challenge.

When I'm in the States, I sometimes go to watch a game. But I don't have many opportunities any more. You can't imagine how I loved sport.

Q: Do you believe that you have reason to fear for your personal safety?

A: Definitely. And the police often warn me that they have found out about a planned action against me. In this respect, the police do a good job.

Q: But where do these threats come from? The Arabs?

A: No. From Jews.

Q: What kind of Jews?

A: Leftist Jews. The media are responsible for inflaming such poison and hatred against me! There must be a dozen leftist Jews who really believe that they would be doing a wonderful thing if they killed me.

Q: Do you know of any particular case, of a serious assassination attempt?

A: No, not in Israel. But in the United States I received a letter bomb. It was a miracle — my secretary got suspicious. Really a miracle! You see, in the United States it's not like in Israel, there was no reason to get suspicious.

There hasn't been a serious attempt here in Israel. I don't know why. Of course, I take steps to protect myself. But if a person is really determined or crazy enough to try something against me, there's nothing I can do to stop him. You can't stop someone who is determined. So I don't sit and worry about my personal safety.

Q: You said a while ago that if the government had the least bit of evidence that you had participated in acts of violence, it would arrest you. The government, however, says that it doesn't want to give you the opportunity for a political trial which would only mean more publicity for you.

A: I think that they're right, from their point of view. I can understand them.

I never cry about what people do to me. In this world, you give and you take. You have to expect occasionally to take blows. That's alright.

Q: Let's get back to the Jewish Defense League. You say it is no longer active?

A: On the contrary, it is active. In November 1984, we organized a large demonstration in America for Jews in the Soviet Union. We blocked the traffic on the streets. And I was arrested. So you see, the League is still active. But not as much as when it was in the news every single day, every single night. There were bombings of Soviet agencies. It was really unbelievable!

Q: So the League will never again be what it was?

A: I don't know. But nothing grows out of a vacuum. The League grew and developed out of a period of activism. The anti-Vietnam War protests, the Black Panthers, etc. This kind of activism no longer exists. Students study seriously. They sit and worry about their pensions. It's terrible, but that's the way it is. And since this is no longer a time for activism, it is not surprising that Jewish students no longer take to the streets. I used to have no problem finding thousands of students to take to the streets. Now to get just 300 is an extraordinary feat. Therefore we have to wait until general conditions improve.

Q: You have been accused of once having planned an attack on the Damascus Gate in Jerusalem.

A: No. That wasn't an attack. I wanted to fix a *mezuzah* to the Damascus Gate. People were furious, of course. But as far as I am concerned, this gate is Jewish.

After the massacre of the Israeli athletes in Munich, I was accused in Israel of having sent out arms and people to attack Libyan embassies. This is correct. We planned to attack the Libyan Embassy in Brussels. The people in charge of this mission did arrive in the Belgian capital, but the ammunition was seized at the airport here. And they arrested me and Paglin, a former member of the Irgun. We received a suspended prison sentence.

Q: *The Israeli government seems to treat you with indulgence. Usually, people who are caught smuggling arms receive a much higher penalty.*

A: I don't believe at all that they are indulgent. Take the Gush Emunim movement, for example. The government is very close to them. Nevertheless, it inflicts heavy sentences on them. To each his paranoia! You never treat people you don't like very correctly! To this day, people here believe that I am an agent of the FBI. Yet I spent one year in prison in the United States. But I won't lower myself to reply to nonsense. The Israeli government has arrested me so many times, so many times. Once they even put me in prison for eight and a half months on an administrative warrant, not even after a trial. You can't say that I am one of their friends.

Q: *In your dreams, how do you visualize the Middle East?*

A: If the Jewish people do what God wants, if they return to Israel, and if they come back to being what God wants them to be, then the Messiah will come. At that time, we'll have peace not only in the Middle East, but all over the world.

Q: *Then there will be no peace before the advent of the Messiah?*

A: No way. We can't have peace any other way. A rabbi once said: 'To deceive other people is a terrible thing, but to deceive oneself is a crime.'

We can't have peace here. The Arabs sincerely believe — and I can understand them — that Haifa belongs to them, and Tel Aviv, and Jaffa, not just Judea and Samaria. They sincerely believe — and, again, I can understand them — that this country belongs to them. In 1948, 80,000 Arabs lived in Jaffa. There were 70,000 in Haifa, and 50,000 in Ramleh and in Lod. They want to go back home. They don't want to go to Nablus. Or to Jericho.* They want to return home. Up until the last elections they believed that they would be able to return home within ten years.

Now everybody is nervous. I have no doubt that I will soon be in the government. And everybody knows that I'm going to have a say in what has got to happen. Everything I'm telling you now, I've been saying for twenty years, and I'll say it again tomorow.

The biggest error would be to believe that once Kahane gets into power, he'll be more moderate; that's not true at all.

I'm bound by the Halacha as much as by the obligation of the Sabbath. Just as I'm not going to stop respecting the Sabbath, I'm not going to stop saying what I am saying to you now.

Q: Some people thought that according to the Cabala the year 1984 was to be an apocalyptic year. What is your opinion?*

A: I'm not making any forecasts. I believe in what I told you before. Who cares whether it's 1984, 1985, 1986 or 1988? What is certain is that very soon terrible things are going to happen, and also beautiful things. I want the beautiful things to happen; I want to prevent the terrible things. Will I succeed? That all depends on the people here.

Q: Do you believe in the wisdom of the masses?

A: There is wisdom and there is stupidity in the masses.

I don't like to generalize. The masses can be intelligent and have a lot of common sense. There is a lot of common sense in people who lead a common, uneventful life. But the masses don't have a lot of imagination. Intellectuals do, but they have very little common sense.

My own life is a mixture of the two. I was raised in a neighbourhood where there weren't many Jews and where I used to fight with non-Jews daily. Later they became my friends. Because when you fight with people, you end up friends. We used to drink beer together. I learned what life is all about, in the streets, and at the same time I went to *yeshiva* and university. I think that's a good mixture.

I'm not a great fan of the masses. I know that they don't have what intellectuals have, but I also know that they have what intellectuals don't have. And I've found a kind of mixture of the two.

Q: You say that you're not a racist, yet you are against mixed marriages.

A: It's not that *I'm* against them. This is the opinion of every single rabbi. The tragedy is that the rabbis don't have the courage to say it out loud, although now it has become a very serious problem.

Q: In what way?

A: It's not only the marriages. There are also many people just living together. Many, many thousands of Jews live together with non-Jews. In every Arab village in Israel, you find Jewish women married to Arabs. According to Jewish law, the children of these couples are Jewish. But they consider themselves Arabs.

The Halacha forbids such unions. Therefore I'm raising a very sensitive issue, because there is a contradiction between Judaism and Western thought. That's what bothers them. When the government proposes its own bill to condemn racism, I'll vote for it. Because I'm against any form of racism. Racism means, for example, that I can say to another person that I am much more important than he is, and that he can never be like me. This is happening right now, in South Africa: when you're black, you can't become white. Therefore, you're inferior. This is what I call racism.

Judaism says: of course we have the truth. God gave us the truth; the Jews are a chosen people. But anyone who wants to be part of the chosen people is welcome. All he has to do is become Jewish. Therefore the government will have to be very careful when drafting this bill. Because Judaism is diametrically at odds with Western democracy, absolutely incompatible.

This is what I tell the government: if you want to condemn Judaism, all right, do it. But don't call it Kahanism. Call it by its right name. But they don't have the courage to do that.

Q: Did you want to go to the Arab town of Taibeh in order to declare war on mixed marriages?

A: Not at all! I didn't want to go to Taibeh. I'm not crazy. I only made this declaration to have all the newspaper reporters go there. I succeeded; they all went there!

Q: What are your intentions concerning all these mixed couples?

A: The problem is not only the mixed couples; I want to get rid of all the Arabs living in Israel.

Obviously, nothing can be done about the mixed couples, except encouraging them to separate. The overwhelming majority of women who have married Arabs are Sephardis. It's only a small number of Ashkenazi★ girls who meet Arabs on college campuses or in the *kibbutzim*. It's a small minority. The overwhelming majority consists of poor Sephardic girls. They are attracted by Arab boys because they have cars, money, etc...

We have to go and tell these girls: your ancestors lived in Morocco for hundreds of years, in Yemen for over 2,000 years, and never during all these years have there been mixed marriages. And here, because of these miserable

79

Ashkenazis — I'm an Ashkenazi — who have been polluted and corrupted by Western democracy, here you have become what your parents and grandparents have never been, now you are doing what your parents and grandparents never did.

The tragedy, I would say to them, if I had a chance to talk to them, is not only what you are doing to your own lives; you have children, so you're not only deciding about your own lives, but about the lives of your children, and the children of your children, etc... It is a chain that goes far back in time, and far ahead. We all are links of the same chain.

Q: You want to punish mixed marriages... ?

A: I want to make mixed marriages a crime. Why should it be alright to punish people who don't pay their income tax? Or people who drive through a traffic light? Mixed marriages are much more important to Judaism than these matters. Our future is at stake.

Take our president, whose name is Herzog. He is so terribly British! There is so little Jewish about him, really! In June 1984, an international conference was held in Israel against assimilation and mixed marriages in the Western world. During this conference, our president came up and spoke against assimilation and mixed marriages. I wrote a letter to him, complimenting him on his magnificent speech and telling him that I'd like to discuss the problem with him and that I would be most pleased if he had the same attitude towards assimilation and mixed marriages in Israel. He answered that he didn't believe that Israel had a problem. I don't like dishonest people like that. I don't care what a person's political views are. If they want to be leftist, that's alright with me; but they should be *honest* leftists!

Q: What kind of punishment would you propose for mixed couples?

A: That's up to the courts and the law.

Q: You must have an idea…

A: It makes no difference whether they get a six-month prison sentence or a 100-shekel fine. What matters is that mixed marriages must be considered a crime. The true problem here is, I say it again, that young Israelis here don't know who they are; they have no identity. They don't know what their jewishness is, because of a secular Zionism which has failed, which has been bankrupt since its very beginnings.

By its very nature, secular Zionism cannot provide any Jew with a reason to be Jewish. At best, it can provide him with a reason to be an Israeli. Which is absurd, as Arabs can also be Israelis. Like anybody else.

Q: Some rabbis who disagree with you admit that the Bible forbids mixed marriages, but they also consider that the Bible is an anachronistic document from a former age, and that you have to move with the times.

A: I have argued with such a lot of rabbis! If a rabbi doesn't believe that the Bible is the word of God, then he doesn't believe in God. He's a 'reformed' rabbi. He should stop talking about the Bible. I don't even know why he calls himself Jewish. Again: a person who doesn't believe in the Bible but insists that he is Jewish is a racist. He should just call himself a human being. Period!

I am not a racist. I am a Jew. How can these rabbis know that such-and-such a rule was good for times past, but not for today? I believe that the Bible is the word of God, and that it is valid for all times. The only people who can argue about the Bible with me are people who believe in the Bible.

Q: Can you tell us how many mixed marriages there are in Israel at the present time?

A: No. According to the Ministry of Religious Affairs,

there are about 7–8,000 mixed marriages with Arabs. In most cases, these are Jewish women married to Arabs. You seldom find a Jewish man married to an Arab woman. This figure does not include the thousands of Jews who are living together with Arabs. And it's going to get worse. Until very recently, it was not at all common practice to have Arabs live in Jewish towns. Today it is very common; once the barriers are broken down, the number of mixed marriages is bound to increase. Many people say: so what? But I say that if you are Jewish, and if you want to remain Jewish, then it's a serious problem.

Q: Some rabbis give different interpretations of the Halacha, especially the former Sephardic chief rabbi of Israel, Yossef Ovadia; they believe that human life is holier than land, and that human life must not be endangered to conquer a hill. What do you think about that?

A: If you follow this logic, we might just as well give up the idea of a Jewish state. Of course, if you want to have peace, there is a very simple solution. Do away with Israel and there will no longer be war.

As a matter of fact, the press has distorted what this rabbi is saying. I know what he is thinking. He has said: 'We don't have the right to give up any land that has been won back. But if it means endangering the lives not only of a few, but of thousands, then it must be given back.'

And I might add the following: how do you know that we would have peace if we returned part of the land? Rabbi Ovadia therefore has spoken in general terms, but he didn't say that we have to give back the land. Of course, human life must be respected. The rabbi says that if we could guarantee that we'd have peace by returning part of the land, then yes, we should give it back. We don't have this guarantee at the present time.

In general I disagree with Rabbi Ovadia with respect to the Halacha. I sent him the manuscript of a book I've written; unfortunately, he answered in the terms you've just mentioned.

Q: Rabbi Yossef Ovadia goes even further. He says that the Israelis should talk with the Palestinians in order to find a solution.

A: I'd talk to anybody, any time. I've always been against Begin's principle of not talking with the PLO [Palestine Liberation Organization].

Q: Is that true?

A: Yes, of course. I'll tell you why. It's very dangerous to believe that the PLO is different from other Arab representatives. As a matter of fact, all of them are pro-PLO. Begin created the concept of the 'moderate Arab'. There are no moderate Arabs. There are clever Arabs and stupid Arabs. Clever Arabs don't say what they mean. I'd love to know what Rabbi Ovadia would have thought had he been in Israel in 1948, when Ben-Gurion proclaimed the state of Israel. Thousands of Jews were killed during the war that broke out afterwards.

Would he have said then what he says today? Again, nothing bothers me so much as the lack of consistency, of logic and honesty in people's minds.

Q: In 1984, the Rabbinic Council cited Rabbi Abraham Yitzhak Kuk, who was in favour of fraternal relations between Jews and Arabs. Wasn't that implicitly condemning you?

A: I don't know what that means. I don't know what he would have said if he had been around during the wars against the Arabs. This brings me back to what I said about people's contempt for the Arabs. The Arabs do not want peace. They want a country. And Zionism is not here to bring peace. It is here to create a Jewish state, and peace, of course, if at all possible. My main objective is a Jewish state, with or without peace.

Anyway, doesn't everybody want peace with the Arabs? I want peace with the Arabs, but on my terms. And the

Arabs also want peace, but on their terms. Their terms and my terms are not the same. And Rabbi Kuk's terms probably weren't the same either. The problem with rabbis is that when they stop talking like rabbis, they start talking like rabbits.

Q: You wanted to go to Hebron to celebrate the assassination of Fahd Qawasmeh [the former mayor]. Doesn't the Bible prohibit rejoicing in the death of others, even if they are enemies?

A: In the Meguila Tractate, the Talmud relates the story of King Ahasuerus: the king called his first minister Haman, asking him to have Mordecai get on the king's horse. So Haman went to see Mordecai, who had been fasting for three days, and who told him: 'I am too weak to get on a horse.' So Haman bent down, and Mordecai kicked him. That's what the Talmud says.

Yes, of course the Bible says not to rejoice over a fallen enemy. But when this enemy is the enemy of the Jewish people, it's a different matter: we have to rejoice, even in their holy places.

Many Jews talk about Judaism although they know absolutely nothing about it.

So, let's talk about Qawasmeh... he was some kind of moderate?! He was a member of the Palestine National Council. You can't call him a moderate, not when his four children wore uniforms on the day of his funeral!

Nobody would have blamed me for proposing a toast to his death if he had been a Nazi. And the Jews, when the Nazi criminals were hanged after the Nuremberg trials, didn't they drink a toast and say: 'Lehayim!' ('To Life')?

My line is honest and clear.

Q: You have said that you respect Khomeini. In what way do you respect him?

A: It's not really a matter of respect. If Khomeini succeeds in combating effectively prostitution and drug abuse, then he is doing a good thing. When he's saying that there shouldn't be anarchy in the world, that's a good thing. But of course, if he then does the horrible things everybody says, then it is a terrible thing.

Q: You said that you are not a racist. Yet, when speaking about the Arabs, you use very racist terms, terms that are offensive. You have said, for example, that Arabs breed like rabbits. Wouldn't you call that a racist term?

A: No! I sincerely wish the Jews would make babies like rabbits. This figure of speech was meant to explain that Arabs make many babies and that it is a threat to us. Pakistanis have many children; it doesn't bother me. God bless them! And if the Arabs want to have many babies — outside of Israel — God bless them!

Q: Before coming into power and being in a position to institute your programme, you probably have a minimum programme. Can you talk about it?

A: The first bill which I presented to the Knesset has nothing to do with the Arabs. Because my first project is to change the school system in Israel, inasmuch as the major part of studies should be devoted to Judaism. This is my main concern. This is the only way to save us and explain to the Jews that they must be Jewish.

As for the Arabs, I would like Social Security matters to be taken out of the hands of the government and handed to the Jewish Agency. It is a private organization and it will make payments only to Jewish people. It's insanity, paying Arabs for making children! The Jews must be clinically insane to have such a system.

I also think that the Arabs should do three years of National Service. Not in the army, of course. But they could build roads, etc. I want to make life hard for them. I want them to think: 'It makes no sense to go on living here; let's take our compensation payment and leave.'

Q: You also want to prohibit non-Jews from living in Jerusalem, and to have segregated beaches for Jews and non-Jews?

A: That's right.

Q: But that's apartheid!

A: No, it's not apartheid. The segregation I propose is restricted to the beaches. I don't want it on the buses, for example. The reason why I propose this bill is that Arabs don't go to the beaches for the sun and for the water, they go there for the girls. Because they can't find any girls in the Arab villages, and Arab fathers won't let their daughters have fun at the beaches.

Q: What about Jerusalem?

A: I have not invented this interdiction for the non-Jews. It's written in the Talmud. You wouldn't believe it, but when I talked about this project, everybody all over the world acted as if Meir Kahane had discovered America! I can't help it if it is written in the Talmud. What can I do about it?

Q: Is it true that you want the Omar Mosque* to be destroyed?

A: I want to move the Arabs out from the two mosques on Temple Mount. The Arabs have no right to be there. Can you imagine what the Muslims would have said if the Jews had gone to Mecca and built a synagogue on the Kaaba, the holy site of Islam? The Temple Mount is not a holy site of Islam; it is the holiest site in all of Judaism. I want the Arabs to get out of there. I don't want to blow up the mosque. But I want them out of there.

Q: But if somebody blew up the mosque, would you applaud it?

A: I certainly would.

Q: What would you say if a non-Jewish state imposed on Jews the same things that you want to impose on non-Jews here?

A: I'd be very happy. I'd even pay them to do it. It's the only way to get the Jews to come here.

Q: Then you approve of the racist measures the Soviets have used against Jews?

A: I sincerely hope they do to their Jews what I want to do to the Arabs. I really wish they would expel all their Jews tomorrow. That's what I shouted at Wilner of Rakah [Communist Party].

Q: But Rabbi Hillel has said: 'Don't do unto others what you don't want them to do unto you.'

A: Yes, he said that. But he was talking about private quarrels, quarrels among neighbours. He wasn't thinking of one people hating another. Besides, if you follow this logic, the Tsahal★ should never bomb Arabs. Because we don't want to get bombed. This is neither the right time nor the right place to apply such rules.

Q: Do you personally resort to violence?

A: Yes. And I have been arrested several times. Outside of Israel, I have been arrested for having bombed Soviet agencies. I have spent one year in prison in the United States.

Q: And what do you think about murders among Jews, for example the killing of Emil Grunzweig, one of the Peace Now activists?

A: Terrible... If he really was murdered. But nobody knows, nobody knows yet; there have been a lot of rumours... But if he really was killed by a Jew, it would be a terrible, a tragic incident; this Jew should be brought to trial and sentenced. You don't do that to a Jew.

Q: In other words, you'd never resort to violence against a Jew? Not even against a communist Jew?

A: If a Jew used violence against me, I'm not sure that I wouldn't retaliate. But we certainly wouldn't be the ones to start using violence against Jews.

Q: A few years ago, a bomb was left in the offices of a Jewish impresario in New York, Sol Hurok; this bomb killed a Jewish secretary. The Jewish Defense League was implicated in this terrorist act.

A: In Jerusalem too, there was the bomb attack on the King David Hotel in 1946, which caused the deaths of seventy Jews. A terrible tragedy, which Begin himself had provoked. Unfortunately, when there is war, certain tragic events can't be avoided.

At the time of the bomb attack you mentioned, I was here, and I learned about the incident through a phone call from America. It was terrible for me. But what can I do about it? Hurok wasn't only a Jew. He was also bringing over Soviet culture to America. A very dangerous culture for us. Because after having seen a performance by the Bolshoi Ballet, you can't have bad feelings for the Russians, because it's so beautiful. And the same is true when you hear the Moscow Symphony Orchestra. The Russians certainly don't send their groups and orchestras to America solely for the artistic pleasure of the Americans. They use them as a political instrument. I met Hurok twice, in 1969 and in 1970. And I told him: you are 86 years old; for once in your life, do something for the Jewish people. You have so much money! You have more money than God could give you... Stop these tours! And he answered with his yiddish accent, his thick yiddish accent: 'I can't do that.'

Therefore, unfortunately, there was that bomb attack. It was not an explosive bomb, it was a smoke-bomb. And I don't know how this poor Jewish girl died. A terrible tragedy. But these things happen! During the last Lebanon war, our own planes bombed our tanks and killed forty Israeli soldiers. It's a terrible thing. What can we do about it?

Q: Is it true that you want the army to execute terrorists on the spot, when they capture them?

A: Definitely! On the spot! On the spot! Right away! Just as we would have done with the Nazis.

I can't imagine anyone getting angry with me if I had ordered Nazis to be killed on the spot during World War II. Terrorists must be made aware of the fate that awaits them when they get caught, and maybe they'll think twice before starting an action. I know these people. I've been in prison with terrorists in this country. (This country is sick — in gaol they put you together with terrorists.) The terrorists were laughing. And I want everybody who is about to commit a terrorist act to know that he will be killed as soon as he is caught.

Q: Do you accept non-religious Jews in your Kach movement?

A: Most voters for my party are not religious. Most members living outside of this city — this is a religious city — are non-observing Jews.

Q: Does that create a problem?

A: If it's not a problem for them, then it's not a problem for me. They accept our programme for certain reasons.

The Jewish Defense League, for example, was open to everybody. Kach is and will remain open to everybody. A Jew is a Jew and I don't care what he thinks.

II

Leading Figures of Far-Right Zionism

In Israel, the term 'extreme Right' does not have the same connotations as in Europe. On the Old Continent it stands for nationalism (and often xenophobia), social conservatism, subversive tendencies, virulent anti-communism, and a taste for uniforms and law and order. In Israel, the extreme Right distinguishes itself principally by its desire to annex the Occupied Territories; other than that, its social programme, its respect for the law and its style differ very slightly, if at all, from those of other political groupings. The rightist parties take their ideological and social principles from the pioneering ideals of left-wing Zionism. This is true of the Tehiya leader Yuval Neeman. It is also true of the Gush Emunim, whose settlements are modelled on the pattern of cooperative villages. What distinguishes the extreme Right is its fundamentalism — or if not fundamentalism, then the preponderant role of religion within it. The xenophobic element — not racism, as has often been suggested — and the cult of violence are also characteristic of some of its members.

Does that imply that all open advocates of the idea of Greater Israel belong to the extreme Right? Not at all. Many of them are members of the two large parties — the Labour Party and Likud — or of the religious parties. In our opinion, the extreme Right comprises only those movements and parties whose principal, if not sole, objective is the creation of Greater Israel. They are all fully or partly religious. They include:

Tehiya ('Renaissance'), the party led by Professor Yuval Neeman. It is the largest, with 5 seats in the Knesset and 4 per cent of the vote. It claims to be a 'mixed' party, with both a lay and a religious membership.

Morasha, the party led by Haim Druckman. It has 2 parliamentary seats and 1.6 per cent of the vote. It is wholly religious in both inspiration and programme.

The *Kach* party of Rabbi Meir Kahane, with 1 seat and 1.2 per cent of the vote. Its programme is exclusively religious.

Gush Emunim, led by Rabbi Moshe Levinger. This is an extra-parliamentary movement. Its followers come from all the extreme-Right, Right and sometimes even Left parties. Practising what it preaches, Gush Emunim is the driving force behind the Jewish colonization of the Occupied Territories. Its political programme is 'ecumenical', and its policy is to cooperate with the government of the day, although this has not always been plain sailing.

The hard core of the extreme Right (Tehiya, Morasha and Kach) currently represents 6.8 per cent of the electorate, and occupies 8 of the 120 seats in the Knesset. In the previous government, only Tehiya was represented, with 3 seats. Thus the extreme Right has moved strongly ahead, mainly at the expense of Likud, in other words, at the expense of the Right. At the last elections, Yitzhak Shamir's party lost 7 seats, going from 48 to 41. Its more extremist followers have deserted it, and most have given their votes to Tehiya, Morasha and Kach.

So the first thing we can say is that, in overall electoral terms, the National Unity camp (Likud plus Tehiya, Morasha and Kach) has stagnated, but at the same time it has adopted a more radical line. The ground lost by Likud has been picked up by the extreme rightist fringe parties, which confirms the saying that when you play the nationalist game, you'll always find someone more nationalist than yourself...

What was more surprising was not that the Right remained stationary, but that it was not defeated as dramatically as political commentators had predicted. When Shamir ran for election in July 1984, he had suffered two serious defeats: a 400 per cent inflation rate that was reducing Israelis' living standards and swallowing up one third of their savings; and the deaths of 600 soldiers in Lebanon with next to nothing to show for them.

This situation, however, did not benefit Labour, which saw the number of its seats fall from 47 to 44. If we include the seats held by Shinui and the Movement of Civil Rights — by tradition close to the Labour Party — the total number of seats held by the Left came to 50... exactly the same as in 1981.

So how do we account for this relative defeat of the Left? The answer is obvious: it was unable to pull in votes from the nationalist-religious electorate. Opinion polls and electoral analyses all came to the same conclusion: the Israeli electorate perceived the Labour grouping as 'too soft on the Arabs'. Israelis were disappointed by the consequences of the Camp David* agreement. They were convinced that the withdrawal from Sinai had achieved nothing, and their feelings of frustration were summed up in the phrase: 'It shows that you can't trust Arabs.' An additional reason for the 'non-victory' of the Labour camp is that it did not set enough store by the Torah, at a time when the country was experiencing a religious upswing. This gives us a second conclusion: religion and nationalism are a crucial stumbling-block for the Left.

Land and the Torah are two ideals close to the hearts of the Sephardic Jews who make up more than half of the

Jewish electorate. The rising Sephardic tide which had brought about Begin's victory in 1977 continued to make itself felt. Fifty-one per cent of Oriental Jews voted for Likud in 1977, 53 per cent for Likud-Tehiya in 1981, and 57.5 per cent for Likud-Tehiya-Morasha-Kach in 1984. The Labour Party obtained 25 per cent of the Sephardic vote in 1977, 22.5 per cent in 1981, and 23 per cent in 1984 (if we include Weizman's Yahad party).

The ethnic divide within the Israeli electorate explains the inverse proportion of Ashkenazi and Sephardic voters for each of the two large parties. A rough estimate shows 70-75 per cent of Likud voters to be Oriental Jews and 70-75 per cent of voters for the Labour Alignment to be European Jews. With ethnic tensions no longer as severe as during the 1970s, the constant improvement of living standards for the Sephardis would certainly have resulted in some of them giving their votes to the Labour Alignment, had they not suffered from the onset of an economic crisis.

In the army, Kach and Tehiya obtained twice as many votes as the national average. The National Unity camp took more than 53 per cent from young people in the armed forces, compared with less than 42 per cent nationwide. This result contradicted those who predicted that the outcome of the Lebanon war would turn Israel's younger generation into pacifists. In fact, it was not because they didn't see the point of their sacrifices in Lebanon that so many young soldiers became such fierce opponents of the war. And the Labour camp is at a loss, because it has no clear answers to offer to the young people who are concerned about their country's fate in the coming years.

It is possible to make a rough calculation of the degree of support for the notion of Greater Israel (Israel plus the West Bank and the Gaza Strip) among the various parties. Among the open advocates (not necessarily all favouring a 'final solution'), we find:

- the extreme Right (Tehiya, Morasha, Kach): 6.8 per cent
- the Right (Likud): 31.9 per cent
- traditional religious parties (National Religious Party (NRP), Shas, Tami): 8.1 per cent.

Thus we find a total of 46.8 per cent in this first category. Taken as a proportion solely of the Jewish electorate, the figure rises to 52 per cent.

If we add the number of Labour voters who support the notion of Greater Israel — a figure hard to estimate, but certainly fairly high — then the proportion of Jewish voters more or less in favour of Greater Israel would easily top 60 per cent.

So we have a third conclusion: one cannot make a clear-cut distinction between advocates and opponents of withdrawal from the Occupied Territories. The line has to be drawn between advocates of an unconditional retreat and pragmatists. This means that the ultra-nationalists are less marginal than their electoral showing might suggest.

1
Tehiya:
an All-Star Party

The word *tehiya* (Hebrew for 'renaissance') is not free of political overtones. It was a calculated choice when Yuval Neeman and Geula Cohen, leading proponents of Greater Israel, took it as the name for the party they created on 8 October 1979, following Begin's 'treason' at Camp David. They were soon joined by members of Gush Emunim and of the Movement for the Land of Israel, and the country's most revered rabbi, Zvi Yehuda Kuk, gave them his blessing.

Political analysts concurred in predicting a bright future for the new-born party. All the odds were in its favour: two brilliant leaders — Neeman and Cohen; an ideal social base — disillusioned ex-Likud supporters; strong back-up in the form of the movements for colonization of the West Bank; and the requisite endorsement by a number of well-known rabbis. Better still, it was the only nationalist party which could boast a combined and co-existing religious and lay membership.

Therefore nobody took it lightly when Neeman declared that his party would gain twenty seats in the 1981 elections. In fact it only won three seats that year, and two more in 1984. But while it has fallen far short of its electoral target, Tehiya remains the largest of the small Israeli parties and the most important in the ultra-nationalist camp.

Neeman had aimed too high. For a newly formed party to have achieved such an outstanding result would have been an unparalleled *tour de force* in Israel's political history. Not least because nobody wanted to be reminded of the struggle against the withdrawal from the Sinai and Yamit (north-west Sinai) which had been Tehiya's principal platform at that time. Leaving aside an uneasiness regarding the true intentions of Shamir's party concerning the Occupied Territories, the only real difference between Likud and Tehiya was that the former still claimed to be in favour of 'autonomy' for the West Bank, as stipulated by the Camp David agreement, whereas the latter saw this as a hidden form of independence. It was too slight a difference to provoke an electoral shift. For that to happen, Likud would have had to be found guilty of a second 'treason'; only then could Tehiya have gained ground.

The second factor in play was the fact that the coexistence of religious and lay members within one party in Israel can never be taken for granted. The resignation of the number three on their list, Hanan Porat, who returned to his former party, the National Religious Party (NRP), almost caused a split in Tehiya. Stripped of its religious component, the party was in real danger of breaking up. Its future and its 'mixed' composition were only secured when Rabbi Eliezer Waldman joined it. Orthodox Jews with beards and young girls in shorts — even when they share a faith in Greater Israel — don't necessarily mix easily.

Yet what defines the party's strength — its blend of remarkable and famous personalities — at the same time seems to explain its weakness. There don't appear to be major conflicts inside the party. But at the time of Hanan Porat's resignation, Geula Cohen seemed tempted to 'return to the fold', in other words, to the Likud. Although its leaders would deny it, Tehiya is a juxtaposition of stances governed by one overriding objective: Greater Israel. Four of the five elected members come from quite different political backgrounds: Neeman from the Labour camp; Cohen from the traditional nationalist Right; Eytan from the army; and Waldman from religious fundamentalism. Their different temperaments add to the contrast: Neeman seems to personify reason, Cohen passion, Eytan strength, and Waldman faith. However, the Tehiya leadership are all agreed on a number of basic positions regarding the Arabs:

1. War is a terrible thing, but it is part of life in Israel. Since they are condemned to a state of quasi-permanent war with the Arabs, Israelis, if they are to survive, must cease considering war as something dirty and immoral.

2. Israel must never withdraw; it must never cede an inch of its conquered territories. To do so would mean engaging in a dangerous dialectic of retreat. Withdrawal from the West Bank today would tomorrow be seen as legitimating Palestinian claims to Galilee and to the Ramleh–Lod area, which are just as 'Arab' and which were also the fruit of conquest (in 1949), and so on...

3. Autonomy for the West Bank and the Gaza Strip would be the prelude to the creation of a Palestinian state; the practice of sustaining hopes among the Arab population by 'keeping the options open' must cease; the annexation of the Occupied Territories must be made irreversible by increasing the number of settlements there.

Within this agreement on basic principles, subtle divergences exist as to the future fate of the inhabitants of the Occupied Territories. Neeman might be pushed to granting them Israeli citizenship, Geula Cohen inclines towards foreign residency status, while Eytan tends to see them as suspects who should be kept under close surveillance. It is a matter of opinion. Since it is not immediately on the agenda, the Arab issue remains an abstraction. The leaders of Tehiya will have to come up with a solution to the problem in order to counter the Labour Party position that a total annexation would entail what Israelis euphemistically call 'demographic risk' — in other words, that the Arab population might one day become a majority in Israel or, at the very least, that 30–40 per cent of seats in the Knesset might be held by Palestinians.

Tehiya has a star-studded leadership, of whom the following are the most notable:

Yuval Neeman: the *Wunderkind*

Yuval Neeman is an Israeli prodigy. A brilliant Jack-of-all-trades, he is the kind of man every Jewish mother dreams of having as a son-in-law.

An outstanding military strategist, brilliant field officer, scientist of worldwide repute, businessman, former minister and party head, Neeman can pride himself on having succeeded in life.

He is a man who should not be judged by his looks. Short and pudgy, at 61 Neeman looks like a small-town businessman. Wearing badly cut grey suits, with an attaché-case in his hand, he is not what one would call the image of a man of passion. He is somewhat reserved, but always polite, and only the clear assurance of his voice betrays the idealist. He is a hard man to interrupt, and he has the self-confidence of an adolescent proudly demonstrating his skill in logic and repartee. Neeman's features are not marked by his age or by what he has been through; this man is not a prey to doubts.

Neeman, an avowed atheist, believes that traditions are important for a revolutionary movement. He strongly defends the spiritual heritage of the Jewish people and preaches a return to biblical sources. Some of his opponents accuse him of being a cynic, playing the religious card in order better to mobilize the masses and win over the rabbis. His mysticism is in fact inherited from the secular Zionism of Israel's founding fathers. In any event, since 1979 dialogue and coexistence with the religious groupings have been the keystone of his political project.

Alongside his mystical view of history, Neeman has a rational concept of the future. No word is dearer to this man of science than 'process'. He does not believe that political formulas can be applied to the present situation. Thus, according to him, the problem of the West Bank is not the demographic imbalance between Jews and Arabs. It is a matter of time. The Palestinians may forget about 'Judea and Samaria', just as they came to forget Galilee. Some of them will emigrate to other Arab countries. If the Israeli leadership leaves no doubt as to its future intentions, then one section of the Palestinians in the Occupied Territories will end up accepting their integration as Israeli citizens or as special status residents. He knows that this part of the world is capable of sudden political upheavals which are hard to predict at the present time. Anything is possible, as long as Zionism can find the space to get its second wind, and can generate a 'renaissance' which will halt the moral decline of Israeli youth. Such a new surge of energy would revive the interest of the Diaspora, who would supply manpower and money for the colonization of the West Bank.

This 'process' may take ten or twenty years. No matter. Neeman plans for the long term. You suggest that his plans are based on a set of gambles:

'But the Diaspora has no reason to emigrate to Israel, and Israel's economic situation is too perilous to permit the luxury of investments in the West Bank...'

Neeman answers: 'You forget what history tells us. If Zionism had been a matter of economic rationalities and the demographic balance between Jews and Arabs, the state of Israel would never have seen the light of day.'

'True, but miracles don't happen twice.'

'All right, let's say that you're right. What alternative do you propose? Do we have a choice? It is impossible to defend Israel when some parts of its territory are barely twenty miles wide. We could possibly live with Arab missiles raining down on Tel Aviv or Haifa, like on London during World War II, but we can't accept the risk of having the Arabs set up camp six miles from some of our major towns, holding a knife at our throats.'

'Yes, but if there was peace, then the borders would no longer be so crucial.'

'Has any Arab regime ever given evidence of its ability to respect a peace? They have a never-ending history of bloody upheavals and social disorder. It would be naive, in fact suicidal, for any Israeli statesman to trust Arab governments. Because of who its neighbours are, Israel is condemned to live dangerously.'

Neeman, strategist that he is, obviously plans for the worst. He strongly maintains that his analysis of the situation is based on geopolitical facts and not on contempt for the Arabs. He says that in no way is he a racist, and claims that he would accept an Arab as a son-in-law, provided, of course, that he adhered to the values of the Jewish state...

He was born in Tel Aviv in 1925, to a family with three generations of *sabras*. On his mother's side, he comes from a veritable religious dynasty in the town of Safad. His grandfather on his father's side had emigrated from Russia at the end of the nineteenth century.

Already at a very young age, Neeman showed talent. He graduated from high school at 15, and had his engineering degree by the age of 20. He devoted his first thirteen years of active life exclusively to the army. In 1945, Neeman enrolled in the officers' training school for the Haganah.★ Mobilized the following year, he took an active part in the 1948-49 war, on the Egyptian front. By the end of Israel's first war, he was already adjutant commander-in-chief of the famous Givati brigade.

During the 1950s, Neeman established himself firmly in the very exclusive circle of strategists who were shaping the future Israeli army. After serving as adjutant chief of operations in 1950-51, he went to Paris to complete his military training. In 1952, he graduated from the Ecole Supérieure de Guerre and the Ecole d'Etat-Major.

Returning to Israel, he took up the very important post of chief of military planning, before moving over to Intelligence. During the Sinai campaign, Neeman held the rank of colonel, and was infantry brigade commander in 1957. He was barely 32 years old. Throughout this period, he was the main force behind the computerization of military planning and operations. He is proud of the fact that: 'Ninety-five per cent of the strategic plans which I drew up during the 1950s were put into effect during the Six-Day War.'

Neeman has never abandoned his first loves: mechanical and electrical engineering. During his time as military attaché in London, he worked for and obtained a doctorate in nuclear physics at the Imperial College of Science and Technology. He subsequently resigned from active military service, but remains an influential member of Israel's military-scientific complex.

By the early 1960s, he was already taking part in Israel's nuclear research programme, and by the mid-sixties he was heading it. In 1964, he attracted considerable attention on the international scientific scene when the prediction he made jointly with Professor Murray Gel concerning the existence of certain subatomic particles was confirmed by the findings of the Brookhaven Laboratories.

Neeman has often been called the 'father of the Israeli atomic bomb', but he disclaims any such paternity with a certain irony: how can the Israeli atomic bomb have a father when it doesn't even exist? At least, not officially... Similarly, he forcefully denies having fathered the nuclear warheads which Israel had apparently planned to use during the October 1973 War. The mystery surrounding his activities in the nuclear field have made him something of a legend. He has figured in a spy story (*The Odessa File*) and in several films, including *Strangeness Minus Three* and *The Way-Out Men*.

Being a renowned member of the international scientific establishment, he is a frequent guest speaker at American, French, Swiss, Finnish, Canadian and many other universities.

From 1970 to 1975, Neeman, who has close ties with the Labour Alignment, was an adviser to Israel's defence ministers, from Moshe Dayan to Shimon Peres. As adviser to the latter in 1975, he resigned in loud protest against the Sinai disengagement agreement between Israel and Egypt. The ultra-nationalist was emerging. In 1976, he quit his post as scientific director at the Ministry of Defence.

Parallel with his official activities, Neeman pursues a busy university career in Israel. He was president of Tel Aviv University from 1971 to 1975, and saved it from bankruptcy. During the three years before he embarked on his political career, Neeman seemed to be devoted to one thing only: his studies. He continued research work in a new field — electromagnetism and the forces at work in the universe of physics.

By 1979, he was becoming increasingly disturbed about what was happening to Israel, and he joined the opposition movement against Begin, whom to this day he considers a 'traitor' (to use his own term), because of the Camp David agreement. He was elected to the Knesset at the head of Tehiya in 1981, and, to everybody's surprise, agreed to join the Begin government as minister of science and development in the summer of 1982. Only three months had passed since the government had ordered the destruction of Yamit before returning the remainder of Sinai to Egypt, a move to which Neeman had been utterly opposed.

Thus the head of Tehiya had decided to bury the hatchet in order to support the war effort in Lebanon. But he made Begin pay a high price for the three precious votes which he gave him — at that time Begin was within one vote of losing his parliamentary majority. As for research and development, Neeman put all his efforts into the project that was dearest to his heart — the colonization of the West Bank. He used part of his ministry's budget for this project, and obtained the go-ahead to build 6,000 new housing units and 7 Jewish settlements in the Occupied Territories. After the 1984 elections, he refused to support a government led by Labour.

Since that time, he has been devoting his efforts simultaneously to science and to party matters, happily 'commuting' between the Knesset and Israeli and American laboratories. He needs action and time for reflection. Research work permits him to 'recharge his batteries', as he puts it. Given the chance, he would devote himself entirely to his research. But the Israeli-Arab conflict is unlikely to be resolved tomorrow, and probably not during Yuval Neeman's lifetime.

Geula Cohen: the *Pasionaria* of Eretz Yisrael

For a woman and a Sephardi to have become Israel's *Pasionaria* is no mean feat. Geula Cohen's advance is all the more extraordinary since it dates from the period when Oriental Jews were systematically excluded from the country's affairs.

Geula Cohen is a Sephardi by her mother Miriam, whose family emigrated from Marrakesh, Morocco, three generations previously, and by her father Yosef, a Yemeni by origin. Moroccans and Yemenis were considered low-class Sephardis in Israel.

Her looks betray her origins: black hair, black eyes, a lithe body, talkative, with a lively temperament which moves quickly from good humour to anger. By no means a tranquil woman. Her biography was published by Gallimard under the telling title *Souvenirs d'une jeune fille violente* (Memoirs of a Young Woman of Violence). Geula

Cohen remains an adolescent who hasn't lost her taste for excesses and occasional provocation. When we met her in Jerusalem in December 1984, she was bubbling over at the prospect of going to light Hanukkah★ candles in the town of Nablus, in the face of opposition from Defence Minister Yitzhak Rabin. However, even her political adversaries — Ben-Gurion used to be one of them — seem to harbour a certain affection for this *enfant terrible* of the Knesset.

Her house on the outskirts of Jerusalem — in occupied territory of course — is furnished like a student's home and decorated with Arab handicraft items. On the walls hang photographs of her only son Tzahi at his Oriental wedding ceremony. After having fought in campus battles with Arab students who sympathized with the PLO, Tzahi has become consultant to the minister for foreign affairs, Yitzhak Shamir.

Geula Cohen was born in 1925 in Tel Aviv, one of ten children. One word was soon dismissed from her vocabulary: 'compromise'. After joining the Betar, the youth movement of Menachem Begin's Herut,★ she became an active member of its armed wing, the Irgun. Shortly afterwards, she left it to join a far more extreme movement, the Lehi. Unlike Ben-Gurion and the majority of the *yeshuv* (the Jewish community in Palestine), Lehi kept up a constant pressure on the British during the war against the Nazis. When, at the age of 16, she had to choose between school and going underground, Cohen had no hesitation. She went underground, and was to become very popular in Israel as a fiery speaker on the Lehi pirate radio station.

She was arrested by the British secret service and given a nine-year prison term; during a first escape attempt she was injured, but she succeeded at the second attempt, disguised as an Arab woman.

In 1949, having married, she went to the Hebrew University in Jerusalem, where she took a degree in philosophy. After fifteen years as a reporter for the newspaper *Maariv*,

Geula Cohen rediscovered her passion for politics. She joined Herut for the second time, and in 1973 obtained the parliamentary seat which she has kept to this day.

Cohen, a mystical but non-practising believer, believes in the Messiah in the figurative sense. As a young girl, she was disappointed that the Messiah's advent did not come with the Declaration of Independence in 1948. When her party, led by Menachem Begin, won in 1977 for the first time in the history of Israel, she again believed that the time had come. She became president of the Knesset's Commission for Immigration and Absorption. But the messiah Begin disappointed her. After Camp David, she once more left the party to join the movement against the evacuation of Sinai. In 1979, she and Yuval Neeman founded the Tehiya party. One year later, she won her place in Israel's history when her bill for the annexation of the Old City of Jerusalem was passed in the Knesset.

Geula Cohen does not believe in tactics and diplomacy. She is interested only in one objective: the restoration of Greater Israel. Her passion for Jewish history and for the Bible is what guides her political ambitions.

Raphael Eytan: Power through Strength

Raphael Eytan has more of a military air than most soldiers. He has the feel of a Humphrey Bogart in some big-budget Hollywood war movie. He is short, solidly built, and dresses like a farmer. And farmer he is; as a member of a *moshav* in northern Israel, he has a small piece of land. In his spare time, he likes to do carpentry, as is evident from his rough hands and dirty fingernails. His bushy eyebrows conceal piercing, suspicious eyes. Eytan is not talkative; his answers are curt and laconic. He is easily roused to anger, but then soon demonstrates a return to cordiality with a hearty slap on the shoulder.

Eytan cannot be called an intellectual. He is not cultivated in the same way as Israel's other military heroes — the likes of Moshe Dayan, Yitzhak Rabin, Bar Lev, and Motta Gur. He was the most widely disputed chief of staff in the history of Israel, and the first head of the Israeli army to prolong his military career by a political career in the ultra-nationalist camp. It was a deliberate choice; most of his predecessors wisely chose the Labour Party.

In fact Rafoul, as he is called by his friends, was the second chief of staff after Motta Gur to have come from a commando unit. He and his predecessor put an end to the uncontested rule of armoured commanders in the IDF. He played a big part in developing the Israeli army's 'look'; Eytan is insolent, casual yet reserved, untidy, loud, and displays more scars than medals. Strongly disliked by politicians, he was loved by his soldiers, partly for his courage, but also because of his indulgence towards soldiers guilty of excesses.

Raphael Eytan, now 56, has fought in all of Israel's wars. At the age of 17, before the creation of the state of Israel, he had signed up in the Jewish underground movement. He fought in the famous 101 Commando Unit which led reprisal attacks against Arabs. This determined the course of his life, and already his courage was legendary.

During the Suez War of 1956, he stormed the Mitla Pass which provided access to the Suez Canal. In 1967, at the head of his Red Berets, he had the thankless task of sur-rounding and capturing enemy fortifications in order to open the way for the IDF's armoured offensive. Eytan broke through at Gaza and took the fortress at Rafah. At the Firdan bridge, he took a bullet in the head. His nephew died at his side; this loss left the only scar which never healed. But this did not stop his progress, and he was the first to reach the banks of the Suez Canal.

Between 1967 and 1973, Eytan led the commandos which terrorized the Palestinian organizations. He was per-sonally in charge of the helicopter raid on Beirut airport in December 1968, destroying thirteen Lebanese planes and causing General de Gaulle's famous fit of temper. He is also said to have led the raid to the heart of the Lebanese capital, in 1973, which resulted in the death of three Palestinian leaders. During the October 1973 War, he was able to head off the initial shock of the surprise attack by Syrian tanks. Eytan, then divisional commander, quickly gathered his forces, and by the time of the ceasefire he had advanced to within a few miles of Damascus. In 1974, he won his first big promotion. He was appointed commander of the Northern Sector, and as such became the architect of Israeli military policy in Lebanon. It was he who armed and organized the Christians in southern Lebanon and, together with his mentor Motta Gur, prepared the ground for the first Israeli invasion of Lebanon in 1978.

Eytan's nomination as chief of operations at General Headquarters in 1977 left no doubt in people's minds that he would soon be given supreme command. Ezer Weizman and Begin, his patrons, had given him the position in order that he could perfect his knowledge of armoured warfare and gain the breadth of experience necessary for a military supremo.

Eytan did not have to wait long. In April 1978, at the age of 49, he was nominated army chief of staff. Political and military circles were somewhat surprised at the promotion. In fact, Begin had deliberately chosen a general who was 'non-political'. Some even went so far as to suggest that Weizman, former airforce chief and defence minister at the time, had favoured this promotion because he did not want to be cast into the shade of his chief of staff. As it turned out, Begin and his ministers had been less than perspicacious. Four years later, in 1982, Eytan and Sharon operated in tandem to impose on Israel the most 'political' of all its wars. The seemingly docile and discreet general saw the truth of what he had always believed — that politicians stand in the way of armies and their victories. In Eytan's opinion, if anyone was to be blamed for the mess in Lebanon, it was Begin. Begin had called him up on a Friday evening in the midst of his campaign and had ordered him to halt his offensive against the retreating Syrian army. 'I only needed four more hours,' he told us, 'only four hours to settle the Syrians once and for all, and to occupy the road from Beirut to Damascus. They were not granted to me.'

With Sharon's complicity, Eytan often disobeyed orders during the Lebanon War. But to be fair, a certain measure of insubordination is tolerated, if not encouraged, in the Israeli army. One of the Tsahal's strong points is the amount of leeway permitted for personal initiative.

If orders had not been disobeyed, the Suez Canal would not have been reached in 1967, Mount Hermon would not have been taken, and Sharon would not have crossed the Canal in 1973, outflanking the Egyptian army which was firmly entrenched behind its SAM missiles. Eytan's error during the Lebanon War was to have exceeded his military prerogatives, to have made decisions that were political.

He believes that he did a good job. He has no regrets and believes that he accomplished his mission, which was to 'destroy the terrorist infrastructure'. If the terrorists ever come back to Lebanon, he claims, it will be the fault of the politicians. As to the tragedy of the Lebanese civilian population, Eytan maintains that as far as possible he fought a clean war. 'We could have left a terrible destruction behind us. But we won without doing it. I prefer not to imagine what would have happened had the Americans been in our place.'

The commission investigating the massacres at Sabra and Chatila charged him with a heavy responsibility for the tragedy, but they made no recommendations for sanctions against him, since he was to leave his post anyway on 19 April 1983, at the end of an exceptionally long term of office.

During the last weeks of his command, this apparently

'non-political' general went on to make frequent inflammatory statements. He moved straight into politics without transition, and very soon unveiled his principal platform: annexation of the Occupied Territories and firmness in dealing with recalcitrant Arabs.

He has often been accused of instigating race hatred, especially when he attributed the murder of a young Jewish girl to an 'Arab terrorist', without producing a shred of evidence. He denies being a racist. But he walks a very thin line separating political cynicism from xenophobia.

Eytan likes to quote Moshe Dayan: 'It is better to have the sword in our hands than at our throats.' However, he adds: 'But against the Arabs on the West Bank we won't need a sword; a stick will do the job.' In his eyes, no Arab can be innocent, since the very foundations of Islam include 'rejection of non-Muslims'. Thus he is in favour of collective punishment, and even argues that Arab parents should be punished for offences committed by their children.

Israel must get used to living with a certain degree of violence. That is the price that has to be paid for keeping the Occupied Territories. According to General Eytan, the evacuation of even a small portion of territory would mean condemning Israel to speedy extinction. 'Well-intentioned people should be more consistent. If it is true that we stole the West Bank, then we also stole the other territories conquered in 1949... ' And so on. As for the Palestinians, to him they are not an Israeli problem: 'It is not for us to solve the Palestinian problem. There are 100 million Arabs; the Saudis have a $130 billion surplus; let them solve it.'

The final step for Eytan, who is not a practising Jew, was to join Tehiya. This he did, and as number two on the party list he entered the Knesset in July 1984.

Eliezer Waldman: Religious Figurehead
Rabbi Waldman is a Tehiya MP and number four on the party list. He represents the party's religious interest. Like

Druckman and many others, he is a product of 'Kukism', a term derived from the teachings of Rabbi Zvi Yehuda Kuk, who had trained a host of Zionist and ultra-nationalist rabbis in his Merkaz Harav *yeshiva*. Before the creation of the state of Israel, Rabbi Kuk's father, himself a highly respected figure, had distinguished himself in the world of Orthodox Judaism by giving his blessing to Ben-Gurion and his atheist pioneers, on the basis that secular Zionism was the first step towards redemption.

For Waldman, it is a matter of divine law that not an inch of the Promised Land be ceded. He compares Israel's governments to the scouts whom Moses had sent to Canaa and who had been very sceptical about the Hebrews' possibilities of conquering the Promised Land. Waldman says: 'In 1967, God gave us a unique opportunity. But the Israelis did not seize it. They did not colonize the newly conquered land. They left all the options open. It's as if they had refused the offer of the Almighty while at the same time thanking him. Therefore God inflicted upon Israel the sufferings of the Yom Kippur War.'

Waldman is not only a religious man, he is also Tehiya's foremost settler. Together with Moshe Levinger, he has created one of the first and most important Jewish settlements on the West Bank, Kiryat Arba, where he lives as head of the Nir *yeshiva*. He was arrested before the elections and held in police custody for several days under suspicion of having been one of the instigators of the attack on the Arab mayors in 1980. Released for lack of evidence, he maintained that the kidnapping of three Israeli liaison officers in Beirut by the Syrians was God's punishment for a government which dared arrest young Israelis accused of having been involved in anti-Arab terrorist activities. His own son-in-law is an active member of the Jewish underground.

Waldman's position in Tehiya indicates the ambiguity of the party's relationship to Jewish terrorism. Neeman himself told us: 'As a party we have to condemn Jewish terrorism, but we cannot prevent members of the party from resorting to terrorism on an individual basis.'

Waldman was born forty-eight years ago in Petah-Tiqva in Israel, the son of Czech parents. As a young child, he emigrated with his family to the United States. He attended religious schools in New York and went on to study philosophy and psychology at Yeshiva University and Brooklyn College.

In 1956, he returned to Israel as a militant of the Bney Akiva, the youth movement of the NRP, and went to work on a *kibbutz* for a year. Not wanting to return to the United States, he signed up at Merkaz Harav *yeshiva*. He then founded a *yeshiva* at Kiryat Arba, which became a hotbed of colonizing rabbis who spread their roots throughout the West Bank and the Golan Heights. He has unusual political views, inasmuch as he fears a polarization in Israeli society between religious and secular groupings. He disapproves of Orthodox Jews who live secluded in ghettos. The logical consequence was to join Tehiya. When a reporter asked him how a rabbi could accept a seat next to such notoriously profane individuals as Neeman, Cohen and Eytan, he retorted: 'A corner of my heart suffers, but there are various degrees to my faith: there is loyalty to the land of Israel, and loyalty to the nation of Israel. I feel at ease with my colleagues in Tehiya because they are devoted to Zionism, to the Jewish people, to the land of Israel, to its social ideals and its pioneer spirit... '

That Waldman is an Orthodox Jew and an ultra-nationalist goes without saying. But the fact that he robs the Left of its monopoly of pioneer ideals is both intellectually disturbing and politically embarrassing.

2
Morasha:
a Gathering Point
for Rabbis

The NRP has been represented in all of Israel's governments since the creation of the state of Israel. It is one of the small parties without whose support (at least until the National Unity government was formed in 1984) no stable parliamentary majority would have been possible. The NRP is also the quasi-official representative of the Orthodox religious community on the political scene. Its members have developed a taste for power, and they are no strangers to politicking and the art of compromise. Involvement in politics has had its advantages. Since it has traditionally controlled the Ministry of the Interior and the Ministry of Religious Affairs, which wield the enormous sums used for financing religious schools and municipalities which respect the Torah, the NRP has been able to set up a structure of veritable fiefdoms.

But in order to maintain this position, it has had to make a number of concessions. In particular, it has had to temper its ardour as regards the question of Greater Israel. Rabbi Zvi Yehuda Kuk condemned the NRP in 1974, when it agreed to join the Rabin government — a government which, in his opinion, was not capable of keeping the holy territories of Judea and Samaria. And political circles were somewhat surprised when, on 12 April 1977, Rabbi Druckman agreed to run for election as the number two

on the NRP list, on the explicit recommendation of Rabbi
Kuk himself. The second surprise was that Druckman was
unknown to political circles in Jerusalem.

Druckman is a frail man with a long beard and the
mischievous eyes of a child. He lacks neither intelligence
nor dialectical ingenuity and is well versed in the commentaries of the Talmud. As director of the Or Etzion *yeshiva*
in the town of Shafir, Druckman sees himself principally
as an educator. He entered politics rather reluctantly, and
to please his spiritual master. In any event, he has no great
political ambitions. In Israel it carries more weight to be
number one in a large religious school than to be number
two in a small political party. Rabbi Haim Druckman was
born in Poland fifty-two years ago and came to Israel via
Romania in 1944 under the auspices of a youth organization. He felt a religious vocation at a very young age, and
studied at the *yeshiva* in Kfar Haroch. He then became one
of the leaders of the Bney Akiva, which sent him as an
emissary to the United States. At the age of 26, Druckman
joined the prestigious Merkaz Harav *yeshiva*; soon afterwards he was nominated director of the Or Etzion *yeshiva*,
which suited him, given his pioneer experiences. Etzion
was neither snob nor stuffy; education there was considered
more important than teaching, and sport and the study of
the Torah went hand in hand.

Despite Rabbi Kuk's reservations about the NRP, he
sent Druckman there with a mission to win Gush Emunim
votes which would otherwise have gone to Likud.
Druckman was elected to the Knesset. But the NRP was
still what it had always been, and the novice MP was
shocked by the cynicism of his party colleagues and the
lack of fervour with which they espoused the ideal of
Greater Israel. In 1981, Druckman was re-elected under
the banner of his own party, the Matzad.

Matzad was a small group of religious people who shared
Tehiya's ideals but refused to share their party with a lay

membership. On the eve of the 1984 elections, Matzad joined forces with Poalei Agudat Israel, a party of much longer standing on the political scene. A religious working-class party, Poalei, like the Labourists, controlled a small network of *kibbutzim, moshavim* and religious schools. From the fusion of Matzad and Poalei Agudat Israel emerged Morasha ('tradition' in Hebrew), headed by Rabbi Druckman. From the beginning, the new party claimed to be a combination of the pioneering movements of the early Israel and of religious fundamentalism. Rabbi Druckman added a personal touch of integrity and idealism.

But Morasha proved unable to achieve what Rabbi Druckman had hoped for — a federation of all the movements, which in total account for about a dozen seats in the Knesset. Paradoxically, it appealed mainly to the religious Right. With 33,000 votes (1.6 per cent of the electorate), Morasha succeeded in winning two seats at the 1984 elections. Rabbi Druckman, modest as he is, left the honour of a position as minister without portfolio in the National Unity government to his number two, Avraham Verdiger.

Unlike Kahane, Druckman, who is a strong advocate of Greater Israel, strongly opposes the expulsion of Arabs from the West Bank. But his objection to Jewish terrorism is just as ambiguous as that of Tehiya. He wants to see a Jewish state governed by the Halacha, and expects to reach his goal through democratic means and through a process of education. Although Druckman is against joining a secular party, he is not opposed to dialogue with the non-religious groupings.

Druckman is a fundamentalist, but he is not a fanatic. He has the patient air of a teacher and his eyes shine maliciously when he scores a point after a long debate. When we interviewed him in his house on a small *moshav* near Ashqelon, in an office piled to the ceiling with weighty tomes, he was constantly breaking off to admonish one of his many children, to discuss some domestic detail with his wife, or to return a call to... Shimon Peres; after which, he picked up, exactly where he had left it, the thread of a very sophisticated line of argument about the holiness of the land of Israel.

3
Gush Emunim:
Spearhead of the
Colonization Movement

'Moshe Levinger, the leader of Gush Emunim, sleeps in a sleeping-bag on the floor of his office in Jerusalem. His activists work day and night, six days a week, twenty hours a day. The offices of Mapam,* though, are always empty. No one works there. At Kiryat Shmona [a low-income development city inhabited mainly by Moroccan immigrants], you never see a single member of our *kibbutz*. The only contact we have with Kiryat Shmona is when we employ its inhabitants to pick our apples. Gush Emunim is much more active in public life than we are. We lead a cloistered life in our *kibbutzim*, occupying the best land at the centre of the country; what right do we have to say that the West Bank has to be given up? Gush Emunim is the personification of what we used to be.'

The speaker is Avital Geva, who is a member of a Mapam *kibbutz*, and a good example of pioneer Zionism, egalitarianism and pacifism. The envy and nostalgia in his voice were indicative of the great changes that have taken place in Israel. The founding myths of Zionism have travelled across from the Left to the Right. This change is best symbolized in the figure of Rabbi Moshe Levinger, who leads Gush Emunim, the principal colonization movement on the West Bank.

Moshe Levinger: 'New Frontier' Adventurer

Just outside Bethlehem, on the road leading to Hebron, a
delivery truck is parked at the side of the road, across from
the Palestinian refugee camp of Daheisheh. Moshe Levinger
has been living in the truck for several weeks and will stay
there, he says, until the government has levelled the camp.
From behind the fence, rocks are periodically thrown at
Israeli cars passing by. It is Hanukkah, and Moshe Levinger
has improvised a *menorah* (candelabra) out of some empty
tin cans; it stands in the middle of a scattering of cheap
crockery, probably identical to that used by his Palestinian
'neighbours'. Inside the truck, a khaki sleeping-bag and a
sub-machine-gun are buried under an indescribable jumble
of objects. A few feet away from the truck, a soldier is
stretched out in the grass, watching over the truck and its
occupant.

For all that he is a long-established practitioner of wildcat
occupations, Moshe Levinger kept dozing off during our
conversation. He was unable to finish a sentence without
falling asleep and we had to wake him up several times to
get a few answers from him. The pressures of his spectacular (or if you prefer, provocative) activities, the leadership
of his movement, his American wife Miriam, their numerous offspring and the study of the Torah leave little time
for rest.

With his lean figure, the deeply lined face that betrays
a life of suffering and tension, and the characteristic beard
of the Orthodox Jew, he is by no means the image of a
leader of a subversive, ultra-nationalist movement. His
thick glasses fail to hide his shyness. He has problems
articulating his thoughts, which are laboriously arrived at.
In short, he is not an ideal 'public relations' man. Yet there
is more to him than meets the eye: he has indomitable
determination and a strong belief in the justice of his cause.
He is convinced that his struggle is paving the way for the
advent of the Messiah. Like many of his kind, his

romanticism and religious mysticism are the product of the Merkaz Harav *yeshiva* under Rabbi Kuk, who was Gush Emunim's spiritual leader until he died.

Convinced that he is in the right, Levinger pursues his course oblivious to its political consequences. Why should he worry, since it is God who guides him in his mad race for the colonization of the West Bank. The course of Levinger's life follows the same pattern as other rabbis of his mould. Born of German parents fifty-three years ago in Jerusalem, he was educated in a religious high school. He served in the Nahal, an elite army unit which combines military training with agricultural work. He had the opportunity to work in a *kibbutz*. He feels a religious and also a pioneer vocation.

After his military service, Levinger was ordained as a rabbi at Merkaz Harav. He became, successively, coordinator of the youth movement Poalei Agudat Israel, rabbi of Kibbutz Lavi, and then, in 1967, rabbi of Moshav Nehalim.

The Israeli army's lightning victory in 1967 provided him with many opportunities. Immediately after the end of the war, he 'squatted' the Park Hotel in Hebron for a period of six months. Transferred to a nearby military camp, he refused to leave it for four years, until he was finally granted authorization to build a Jewish settlement in Hebron — Kiryat Arba, which to this day is the most important Jewish settlement on the West Bank.

His appetite for colonization is insatiable; he has been responsible for setting up Camp Horon, Sebastia, Qadum, Elon Moreh and others. In 1979, Levinger, together with seven other families, occupied a former Jewish turn-of-the-century dispensary in Hebron's town centre. His dream was to rebuild the old Jewish quarter of Hebron, which was destroyed during a pogrom in 1929. He was also in the vanguard of the colonization movement which tried in vain to resist the destruction of Yamit by Begin's government.

All Israeli governments, whether Left or Right, have succumbed to his pressures. Not that they were opposed to establishing settlements, but they would have preferred them in areas with fewer Arabs, closer to large Israeli towns, and following a rational plan. Levinger has little time for the complicated computations of bureaucrats and diplomats anxious for the future of Israel. For him, the West Bank is a 'new frontier'.

Parallel with his colonizing activities, he periodically sets off on pilgrimages through South Africa and the United States in order to stir the spirit òf migration in the Diaspora. Because what the country needs most is neither space nor money but... Jews.

When you suggest to him that his policies are killing any hope of peace with the Arabs, Levinger replies: 'No. The advance of the Jewish people, the fulfilment of the Redemption, of the morale and integrity of the Jewish people and of Eretz Yisrael — these are more important than any hypothetical peace. It is through all this that the world will have peace.'

'Enlightened' rabbis deride his fetishism for 'dust and holy stones'. They believe that it is more important that the Jewish people return to the path of an honest religious life, to *teshuvah* ('being born again'). Levinger replies that the fulfilment of Greater Israel is just as sacred a duty as respect for the Sabbath.

Levinger denies harbouring racist feelings for the Arabs. For him it is a religious obligation that 'goys' be respected. The Palestinians' civil rights must also be respected: they should even have the right to Israeli citizenship, on condition that they also accept the obligations it entails. But 'friendly' coexistence with the Arab population has to go hand in hand with a very firm attitude towards 'terrorists and troublemakers'. The whip must not be put back in the cupboard.

The fact that, under this policy of 'firmness', democratic

ideals take a severe battering does not disturb Rabbi
Levinger, to whom democracy is not the most precious
value of Judaism ('Jewish national renaissance is more
important than democracy. You can no more democrati-
cally suppress Zionism, the Law of Return and colonization
than you can forbid people to breathe or speak.') Rabbi
Levinger respects the country's laws and institutions, but
he regards certain other principles as more sacred. When
he approved of, or participated in, reprisal attacks against
the Arab civilian population, was he acting against the law?
The police thought so, and arrested him in July 1984 during
an investigation into Jewish terrorism. He was released,
though, for lack of evidence.

Many of Levinger's friends have resumed their studies
in *yeshivas* or have chosen the more comfortable surround-
ings of the Knesset. Levinger, though, pursues his mad
race, with his three inseparable companions by his side:
his prayer book, his sleeping-bag, and his machine-gun.

Redemption Zionism

One day in May 1967, exactly twenty days before the
Six-Day War, the *yeshiva* Merkaz Harav was, as usual,
celebrating Independence Day. Rabbi Zvi Yehuda Kuk was
making his usual speech. Year after year he sang the praises
of the state of Israel. This time, however, something
strange happened: his audience started to cry. The rabbi
had changed the tenor of his words. He accused the nation
of being content with an Israel that was mutilated, crippled,
without its holy cities of Hebron, Nablus, Jericho and so
on. 'We have sinned,' he concluded. When, less than a
month later, the Tsahal took Hebron, Nablus and Jericho,
religious opinion was convinced that Rabbi Kuk must be
a prophet inspired by God.

People started wearing the *yarmulka* as a symbol of their
devotion to Eretz Yisrael. Only the Orthodox Jews of Mea
Shearim★ still held to their view that Israel was the work

of Satan, and remained secluded in their ghettos. At last Zionism and religion had been reconciled, and the rabbis took to the streets to make their mark on the country's political scene.

The Labourists had just presented Israel with its biggest military victory yet, and its most extensive territorial conquests, but paradoxically they did not know what to do with them. While the Left was still in a position to do so, it offered to trade the territories in exchange for peace. But the Arabs slammed the door in their faces by their triple refusal at Khartoum: 'no' to peace, 'no' to direct negotiations, and 'no' to recognition of the state of Israel.

The rabbis seized the torch of pure, hardline Zionism out of the hands of the exhausted pioneers who now proved unable to carry through their victory. Many young Israelis saw them as Israel's second chance. The 'black beards' saw themselves as combining religion with the spirit of Ben-Gurion's pioneer Zionism and Begin's ultra-nationalism. The Torah filled the gap left empty by the great leftist disillusionment of the 1970s, and the fact that Zionism as originally conceived had run out of steam. It is true to say that a religious Zionist party did exist — the NRP. But classic and conservative though it was, the NRP allowed itself to be swept along with the new trend. The war of 1967, which had transformed people's fears of a new holocaust into a brilliant victory, and the 1973 war, which had highlighted Israel's isolation, had led many to believe that the time of the Messiah had come.

This led to the emergence of what some have called 'Redemption Zionism'. This is founded on a sort of holy trinity: the Land of Israel, the People of Israel and the Torah of Israel. Hanan Porat, one of the movement's ideologues, has written: 'Working in a settlement is a spiritual uplift, an antidote to the materialism and permissiveness which have swept the country. This is why the leadership of this country has passed from the secular into the national-religious camp.' Opponents of this ideological trend have dubbed it 'Kulturreligion'.

This trend has frightened moderate rabbis like those of the Oz Veshalom★ ('Fortitude and Peace') movement as much as those of the Diaspora, among them the chief rabbi of Great Britain, Immanuel Jakobovits. For them, the mixing of religion and politics is contrary to Jewish tradition, and results in a corruption of both. They object to the movement's idolatry with regard to land, and they proclaim that men's lives are more sacred than the hills of Hebron. Moshe Levinger, Meir Kahane and the others are seen as the kind of false messiahs that have appeared regularly throughout Jewish history.

Gush Emunim retort that the Promised Land was God's gift to the Jewish people; it belongs not only to the present generation, but to future generations as well. Therefore it cannot be the object of negotiation, let alone a referendum; this would be tantamount to taking a vote on whether to respect the Sabbath.

The two camps seek to justify their views by citing unimpeachable biblical references. 'Enlightened' rabbis and 'Orthodox' rabbis represent two trends within Judaism; in the Bible there exists both a spiritual and a martial tradition. Gush Emunim, in the close way it links the land, the people and the religion of Israel, tends to provide the literal reading, while its opponents refer more to the spirit of the texts.

Gush Emunim claims not to be party political. The movement is not a political party and does not put up candidates for the Knesset. Gush Emunim's political creed is as follows: Greater Israel is not an issue for the political parties. It is a non-partisan problem and Gush Emunim does not engage in partisan activities. 'Our dialogue is not with those who struggle for power, but with the nation.'

The Bloc of the Faithful was officially set up at a conference in February 1974, during which the delegates decided to cease being a pressure group within the NRP, in order to become independent. Rabbi Haim Druckman came up with the name Gush Emunim. The split had been expected. After all, Yosef Burg, leader of the NRP and at that time minister of the interior, had publicly admitted his doubts as to the imminent advent of the Day of Redemption. He had also questioned the necessity of sacrificing the lives of soldiers in order to keep territory.

During the summer of 1974, Gush Emunim organized its first spectacular action. One day after Rabin became prime minister, it set up the unauthorized Horon camp. But although the movement emerged formally in 1974, its principal leaders and militants had already been active for a long time previously. They had their own temple, the Merkaz Harav *yeshiva*, and a high priest, in the shape of Rabbi Zvi Yehuda Kuk. From the beginning, the position as chief of operations was taken by Moshe Levinger.

Moshe Levinger and his Bney Akiva followers have been active in the West Bank since 1967. Granted, they were not the only ones. The Movement for the Land of Israel, created right after the Six-Day War by a group of writers, university academics and politicians, has provided support for young people from the *kibbutzim* who embark on establishing settlements. The non-religious groupings at that time had a preference for the Golan Heights: the first colony was established there on 15 July 1967. Situated to the east of Quneitra, it was named Kibbutz Merom Hagolan, and had links with the the left-wing pacifist party Mapam. Mapam limited itself to building settlements on the Golan Heights; the Labour Party, on the other hand, created twenty settlements throughout the Occupied Territories.

At the start, Gush Emunim recruited its members mainly from among the young people of Bney Akiva. It went on to win an enthusiastic following from young soldiers in elite army units, and their presence served to radicalize the movement. Without their *yarmulkas*, they could easily be mistaken for militants of the Peace Now movement. Thus

Gush Emunim attracts not only the faithful; it also attracts members of *kibbutzim* or *moshavim* who want to participate in the adventures of Greater Israel, in the colonization of Arab lands — people who believe firmly in the integrity of the movement's leaders, even though they may not share all their religious ideas. Moshe Levinger and his colleagues seemed to be the only people in Israel willing to practise what they preach. As a result, their followers have come to see them as quasi-prophets, come to save Israel from moral decadence and corruption.

Prosperous Jews from the cities, industrialists like Ernst Wodak and Israel Shakar, and American 'friends' have inundated Gush Emunim with offers of money, construction materials, machinery and new technology. This has enabled it to create not only agricultural colonies, but also a sizeable industrial development on the West Bank. Gush Emunim has the political support of all the parties on the extreme Right (Tehiya, Morasha and Kach), and on the Right (Likud), but owes allegiance to none of them. Although it claims to be anti-establishment, it is far from rebellious in relation to the established authorities. Gush Emunim collaborates with the worldwide Zionist movement in order to encourage immigration (*aliyah*).* It is an attractive showcase for young Jews in the Diaspora looking for ways to get involved.

The widespread belief abroad that most of these settlements have been created without the government's approval is wrong. In fact, at the start, most of the settlements beyond the 'Green Line' (the pre-1967 border) had been set up under Labour governments. Following the Allon plan (named after the then minister of labour), they were strung out along the valley of the River Jordan. They were simultaneously agricultural settlements and military outposts. Moshe Levinger was able to exploit personal rivalries within the Labour Party in order to achieve his goal, which was to create his own settlements. At Kiryat

Arba, he was able to counter the opposition of Moshe Dayan by mobilizing Yigal Allon in his support — his first supporter was a leftist. At Ophra, he played Rabin off against Peres, and at Qadum Qedumim, Peres against Rabin... His relations with the Begin and Shamir governments were a little better, but not much.

As a matter of fact, Gush Emunim's attitude to all governments has been to pursue a policy of *fait accompli*. It establishes settlements which are 'illegal', but which then receive the government's blessing and financial support.

Increasing Jewish terrorism in the Occupied Territories compelled Yitzhak Shamir to arrest a number of Gush Emunim militants. According to the police, these militants received the blessings of rabbis before going out on their sorties. But the fact that Israeli public opinion has reacted strongly against Jewish terrorism — together with the sentences handed out to those involved — seems to have reduced the killing of innocent Arabs. Even members of Gush Emunim have condemned these killings. After the assassination of the Jewish pacifist Emil Grunzweig by another Jew, there were real fears that Arab terrorism might give way to a deadly conflict between Jew and Jew. Both Gush Emunim and Peace Now made efforts to avoid such an escalation. The leaders of the two movements met to discuss ways of lowering the tension. The spectre of civil war hangs over Israel. But all the ultra-nationalist movements, including Kach, agree that there is a limit beyond which they will not go, even if it means occupied territories having to be returned: Jewish blood must not be shed. In the event of part of the West Bank being handed back, they envisage organizing passive resistance or mounting a movement of civil disobedience, but they draw the line at armed conflict.

So, are there reasons to be afraid of Gush Emunim? Outside its ideological influence, where does its real strength lie? There can be no doubt that it is a professional, influential and well-funded organization, quite unlike the amateur efforts of Peace Now. It employs about twenty permanent staff, publishes its own literature, and finances missions abroad. Gush Emunim is run by a thirteen-person secretariat which delegates the administration of daily matters to a small group of men, who include Moshe Levinger, Hanan Porat, Nathan Natanson and Israel Harel.

There are 25–30,000 Jews living in the one hundred and fifty settlements established in the Occupied Territories; more than half of these are located on the West Bank and Gaza, with the rest to be found in the Jordan Valley and Golan Heights. Of the one hundred and fifty settlements, thirty are affiliated to the Amanah network which is the most important grouping and is controlled by Gush Emunim. In these thirty settlements lives more than half of the Jewish population of the Occupied Territories, and two thirds of these are children. This is perhaps not much to show for eighteen years of colonization. These figures are no great credit to Gush Emunim. In fact, the movement seems to have reached its peak, as far as human resources are concerned. Since its missionary efforts abroad have brought scant results, Gush Emunim is now trying to foster an 'internal *aliyah*', in other words a migration from within Israel's pre-1967 borders, into the Occupied Territories. It has created a community *yeshiva* in the development town of Kiryat Shmona in Galilee, in order to encourage the faithful.

But while some Israelis may be willing to move into the Occupied Territories, their object is generally to install themselves in comfortable houses on the outskirts of Jerusalem, or at the very least within half an hour's commuting distance of Tel Aviv. Furthermore, if this 'internal *aliyah*' is at all successful, it is likely simultaneously to bring about detrimental consequences. For example, if large numbers of Jews were to move out of Galilee — where half the population is Arab — this would cause demographic imbalances in 'lesser' Israel, at the expense of dubious gains on the West Bank.

Gush Emunim's strength, like that of the *kibbutzim*, is principally ideological. It is worth remembering that only 2 per cent of the population belong to this flower of Zionism.

Its settlements are organized along communal lines. All members have equal rights and duties. Although not always the case, in most instances the houses are modest. What it costs Gush Emunim to establish their settlements is ten times less than what it costs the Jewish Agency which oversees the absorption of new immigrants. Workshops and factories often have a cooperative structure, although private ownership is also accepted. The settlements are not meant to be treated as dormitories for their members. Everybody shares in the work, and if necessary they may give up former jobs in the towns. Many settlements have their own schools and dispensaries, and even absorption centres for new immigrants. With the exception of a few 'mixed' ones, all the settlements are religious.

Although they form a network which to a large degree provides for its own defence and is not controlled by any party or by the police, most Gush Emunim settlements could not survive economically without government help. As a matter of fact, it takes a fair portion of idealism to live in them, and this is both the movement's strength and its weakness. Many young Israelis applaud Gush Emunim's devotion, but they are not prepared to submit to the rigours of its communal life style.

For Gush Emunim, populating the West Bank with Jews or building a viable economy there is not the main objective; they are working to expand the number of settlements, however small, to the point where territorial compromise becomes impossible. Where others speak in terms of economics, they speak of geography or geopolitics.

Some believe that they have already succeeded. Even

before the withdrawal from Sinai, Rabbi Yoel Ben-Nun was saying: 'Even the doves have to admit that we have annexed one and a half million Arabs: Arabs from Israel, from East Jerusalem (which is never going to be given back), from Hebron (including the Etzion Bloc), an enclave which nobody will return; the same is true for the Gaza Strip and the Rafah Gap... We have annexed all these regions *de facto* or *de jure*. Therefore *the problem is only with 300,000 Arabs from Samaria*, and even fewer if we deduct those from Ramallah, which some doves are refusing to give back. How can anyone believe that giving back Samaria would solve the problem? To be completely "realistic", we would have to give up Galilee and its Arab population as well.'

In this light, it is easy to see how the territorial compromises proposed by the Labour Party would be a nightmare for the poor diplomats and planners whose job it would be to trace a new border. But, reply the doves, if there were to be a territorial compromise, it is not impossible that Jews could live peacefully under Arab sovereignty, just as there are Arabs living under Israeli sovereignty. The precedent of Yamit, however, does not really justify such optimism.

Its opponents say that Gush Emunim's error is to believe that they can establish an irreversible situation by dotting the West Bank with a host of tiny settlements. The facts argue against it: this movement is not going to overturn the overall geographic or demographic balance. From the geographic point of view, only 6 per cent of land on the West Bank can be considered as 'available'. Anything more than that would have to be expropriated from the Arab population *manu militari*, and no Israeli government can envisage embarking on this option on a large scale.

As to the demographic ratio, even if one accepts the most optimistic assessments (that the balance has remained the same inside Greater Israel since 1967 — 63 per cent

Jews and 37 per cent Arabs), there is little expectation that it is going to shift in favour of Israeli Jews.

The official objective, as defined by the Shamir government and still valid to this day, is to achieve a Jewish population of 100,000 in the Occupied Territories within the next three to four years. By now everybody in Israel knows that this target will take up to ten years to achieve. Settling a single family costs $100,000, which means that $2 billion would be needed to bring in 20,000 more families. To achieve these targets in the short term would mean imposing a draconian austerity on the people of Israel. Theoretically it can be done, but it is likely to result in a large-scale emigration of Israelis to the United States and Europe in search of better living standards. Squaring of the circle, in a way...

Gush Emunim's objective of settling one million Jews on the West Bank before the end of the century is considered utter political fiction by its adversaries. It would require an investment of $200 billion! Gush Emunim's dreams, together with the government's own projects, run up against two insuperable problems: lack of money and lack of Jews. Unless all Israelis agree to turn themselves overnight into settlers and cowboys... or the USSR decides to donate all its Jews to Israel... or a wave of persecution of Jews sweeps the Western world... Too many unknowns, by far.

Even if we assume that the target of settling 100,000 Jews in the Occupied Territories could be attained quickly, this would still not improve the ratio above the 1:13 mark, given that 1,300,000 Palestinians live on the West Bank and Gaza Strip. And according to commentators, this would not be enough to dissuade any government from returning portions of the West Bank, however small. Besides, the distinction between hawks and doves is not particularly useful when it comes to territorial matters. After all, it was the doves of the Labour camp who conquered the territory in the first place, and it was the hawks of Likud who gave back the biggest part of it (Sinai).

The Arab population of the West Bank has learned its lesson from the events of 1947. They are not going to leave of their own free will. Nor is there any chance that the Israelis will agree to adopt the programme envisaged by Meir Kahane. Granted, some war whose contours cannot as yet be foreseen might force the Arabs once again down the road to exile. But it is unthinkable that the international community, and in particular the United States, would tolerate another large-scale Arab exodus.

It is equally obvious that most Israelis are unanimous in refusing to have a Palestinian state set up right on their doorstep, and an Arab army camped twelve miles outside of Tel Aviv. For them, any question of a simple return to the 1967 border, even for the best of strategic reasons, is unthinkable.

One Gush Emunim leader declared, with a touch of irony: 'I am a dove — I'm not after the East Bank of the Jordan.' But he added seriously: 'I hope that we'll get it some day, though.'

Strategists and pragmatists view the frontier problem in terms of defendable borders: the advocates of Greater Israel see it in terms of Israel's historical borders. But neither the one nor the other can be precisely defined. Perhaps this is only to be expected. If there is one thing on which everyone agrees, it is that the Jewish syndrome is very much a frontier syndrome. After all, they point out, the word 'Hebrew' is derived from the root 'to pass'.

III

To Be Jewish...

To be or not to be... Jewish. Certainly, that is the basic question for Rabbi Meir Kahane, since the answer to it determines the entire course of his thinking. Can we be so sure that the strong aversion, the hatred and the fears that his statements arouse in Israel are inspired by a pure democratic spirit of anti-racism and anti-fascism, and not by a nagging anxiety, brought about by the resuscitation of a question that is as old as the Bible? Kahane, after all, is Jewish himself, and a rabbi into the bargain. And if anti-Semitism has not been totally eradicated, is not he himself as likely to be a target?

What is a Jew? One might recall the words of Jean-Paul Sartre forty years ago, immediately after the Years of Horror, when he stated: 'A Jew is a man whom others take for a Jew; this is the simple truth from which one must start... It is the anti-Semite who *makes* the Jew.' In making this statement, which served as a reference-point for a whole generation of leftist intellectuals, the great French philosopher unwittingly revealed himself to be more anti-Semitic than the anti-Semites described in his essay.

It would be more correct to say that he appears as such *today* when we view his ideas in the crude light of the opinions articulated by Meir Kahane. When Sartre wrote the above, *juiverie* (a difficult word in French, unlike the current Anglo-Saxon usage 'jewry') was denied, negated, in good faith, and as a product of Enlightenment philosophy. Only virulent anti-Semites could have used such a term. Sartre also wrote: 'For an anti-Semite, what makes a man a Jew is the "jewry" perceived in him, this "jewry" being a principle analogous to the qualities of a phlogiston or the soporific virtues of opium.' In other words, for people who are not anti-Semitic, *juiverie* ought not to exist.

Kahane has his own way of answering this question: 'The only reason to be Jewish is the Torah. There is no other reason. Anyone who was born Jewish, sure, he's a Jew. But he's not a good Jew if he doesn't respect the Torah.' In short, jewishness is based not so much on race but on divine law. And this divine law is not racist, for all that it does not fit into the philosophers' terminologies. Indeed, a non-Jew can become a Jew, provided he converts to Judaism and joins the 'Chosen People'.

This said, Kahane has harsh words for Jews who do not believe in God; he even accuses them of racism. Not without a degree of justification, one has to admit. Because if Judaism is not founded on God, then what else can it be founded on apart from race? 'The biggest racist', he asserts, 'is the Jew who doesn't see that to be a Jew is something special... The biggest racism would be to create a Jewish state that isn't Jewish, which is not ruled by the Torah. Because', he repeats, 'the only thing which distinguishes Jews from non-Jews is the Torah.' Therefore to call Kahane a racist would be tantamount to saying that Judaism is racist.

Now, God ordered his people to live in Israel. He not only delivered them from slavery in Egypt; he also gave them a country: the Promised Land. It is a 'miserable' place, 'uninteresting', an 'absolute disaster', but for Jews it is a holy commandment that they live there. Otherwise, 'what would be the point of being here?' asks Rabbi Kahane — not a man to mince words. After all, it's hardly the living standards in Israel that attract Jews from the Diaspora, especially not if they are Americans, like Kahane.

Therefore one's reason for being Jewish and one's reason for living in Israel have a common root: divine law. Here again, Kahane finds fault with secular Jews. For Kahane, 'the great insanity of Zionism' was to have wanted to set up the state of Israel for the sole reason that Gentiles refused to allow the Jews to assimilate. In other words, had the Jews been given the opportunity to assimilate, the state of Israel would not have been created. Kahane is convinced that this kind of Zionism — the Zionism of Herzl and the founding fathers, of Ben-Gurion, Golda Meir, etc — was 'bankrupt' from the start because 'it cannot provide any Jew with a reason to be Jewish. At best, it can provide him with a reason to be Israeli, which is absurd, since anybody can be an Israeli... '

So it is a divine commandment that Jews, *all* Jews, live in Israel. 'God does not want Jews to live in a foreign country. He wants them to return home. If they refuse to return home, a great tragedy may come upon them,' he thunders, as he prophesies that, fanned by the world economic crisis, a new wave of anti-Semitism is about to sweep the world, and that it will go far beyond the horrors of Hitler's Germany. In a sense he would almost welcome another wave of anti-Semitism, since this would force the Jews to obey God and go to Israel. He would also like the Soviets to expel all Russian Jews 'tomorrow morning', in the same way that he wants to expel the Arabs. But, he emphasizes, that divine commandment only has meaning if the state of Israel is ruled by the Torah.

What would be the borders of such a state? They are inscribed in God's book — in other words, the Bible. Thus Eretz Yisrael includes all of the northern part of the Sinai, up to El Arish; it takes in part of Jordan, sections of Lebanon,

Syria and Iraq, and stretches as far as the River Tigris. But wouldn't this mean perpetual war with the Arabs? Answer: peace is not a question of where the border is set; besides, the Arabs are not going to agree to any borders anyway. They never have and they never will.

Racism? Once again, Kahane is ready to defend himself. The true racists are those left-wing Jews who despise the Arabs enough to believe that they can 'buy' them by raising their living standards and sending them to university. The fundamentalist Kahane claims to know the Arabs better than his progressive compatriots. In his opinion, the Arabs are a proud people; they see this as their country, and they would not want to live under Jewish law, even if this meant bringing them prosperity and education. 'When certain Jews say to the Arabs: "Look what we've done for you, all the good we have done... We found a desert here and we transformed it into a garden," the Arab replies, with good reason: "This may be true, but it was my desert and now it has become your garden."' In his opinion, left-wing Jews behave like naive colonizers; what is worse, they suffer from bad conscience: 'The Left in Israel', he says, with a degree of malice, 'believes that it is not entirely natural for Jews to be living here in Israel.'

Kahane himself is free from any such bad conscience. He understands the 'pride' of the Arabs so well that he wants to drive them out of Israel. 'Because', he says, 'there is no such thing as an innocent Arab.' Being nationalists, 'good Arabs', meaning true Arabs, inevitably have to be against the very existence of the state of Israel — there is no such thing as 'moderate Arabs' on the one hand and Arab PLO militants on the other. Like the French under the Occupation, there are brave men and less brave men. Not all of them throw bombs, but all of them hate the people who have occupied 'their' country. And the more educated they are, the longer they have studied, the more revolutionary they become. Therefore they must be expelled, either by financial inducements, or, if necessary, by force. And better to do it today than tomorrow, because given the way the demographic ratio between Jews and Arabs is developing, Israel will not have the means to do it tomorrow. In any event, as of today, the time has come to start frightening the Arabs, so that they realize that time is no longer on their side — that Jewish colonization is an irreversible fact of life.

At this point, one might have the impression that Kahane has taken leave of his senses. But his bizarre utterances have a certain logic. In the beginning, God promised the Jewish people that he would give them *this* land, in order to build not an American- or a French-style democracy, but a Jewish state ruled by Jewish law. How could Arabs exist as fully fledged citizens in such a state?

Without embarrassment, Kahane points to one of the most flagrant contradictions of the Israeli state as presently constituted. He counters those who call him a fascist: You claim to be democratic and secular, but one of the laws which you accept is neither democratic nor secular. It is, furthermore, the law on which your state is built: the Law of Return, which applies solely to Jews. You are blind to the future; when changing population patterns mean that the Arabs become a majority in this country, and they abolish the Law of Return, will you still be so democratic and secular? And when this state has an Arab majority, with Arab laws — because the Arabs won't have your complexes — will you still be so democratic and secular? And when that Arab majority decides to throw out the Jews, will you still be so democratic and secular? You are also blind when you tolerate mixed marriages. For centuries, the Torah has barred Jews from marrying non-Jews. And in today's Israel, young Arabs exempt from military service seduce your daughters while their sisters have to remain secluded in their homes. And you're also blind, he would say, to the point of collective suicide, when you have a democratic and secular social security system which pays Arabs so that they can breed like rabbits.

Kahane's formidable 'intelligence' consists precisely in the fact that he questions the very legitimacy of the state of Israel. History cannot provide this legitimation. 'Who cares whether the Jews lived here 2,000 years ago?' he asks, with reason. Democracy does not provide a legitimation either, because once the Arabs become a majority, the Jewish state will cease to exist, and there will probably be no Jews left in Israel. Legitimation cannot be via racism, since Judaism is not racist. And least of all can it come via nationalism: 'I am not a nationalist,' he claims. 'The Jews are a nation only by the will of God. Why should I go to war for one flag rather than another? It's insane.' There can be only one legitimation for Israel — divine law. And if you do not accept this legitimation, what are you left with to build on, other than historical claims that are without foundation; or a purely formal and *ad hoc* democracy — false and hypocritical; or tacit forms of fascism or racism which will ultimately lead to the ruin of the state which you have built and which you claim to be defending? Because once again, the only possible justification for the state of Israel is divine law. The fact that the country won't admit it shows how 'sick, intellectually sick' it is, a prey to lies, double-talk, excessive conservatism, fascism and racism; and in the long term, condemned by its own contradictions.

All this explains why Rabbi Kahane inspires fear in Jews, both inside and outside Israel. He proclaims *urbi et orbi* the specificity of Judaism, which the rationalism of Enlightenment thinking had glossed over, yet which is essential to any understanding of the 'Jewish question'. This specificity is the relation, willed by God, between a particular people and a particular piece of planet Earth. All other religions have 'holy sites'; none has a Holy Land. However small the Promised Land may be, compared to the Persian,

Greek, Roman, Arab, British, American or Soviet empires which have surrounded it, however poor it may be in natural resources, the Promised Land is still too vast, intolerably so, because it was promised by God to *his* People. 'For centuries, we have prayed three times a day in order to be able to return to this country.'

This reminder embarrasses Israeli Jews, to put it mildly; a solely secular version, however democratic, of this specificity of the Jewish religion can at best only be nationalist. It is equally embarrassing for Jews in the Diaspora, because it implies (and not so implicitly, when articulated by Kahane) that they are disobeying God's commandment when they choose to live anywhere other than in Israel. Kahane deliberately reverses Sartre's statement when speaking of Judaism: it is not the anti-Semite who makes the Jew; it is rather that the Jew plays into the hands of the anti-Semite.

Kahane shocks Jews both inside and outside of Israel, not only because of the vigour and the calculated crudity of his utterances — grist for the media mill — but also because he refutes Sartre's negation of jewishness, which in fact had quite suited everyone, Jews and non-Jews alike. 'The only relation that Jews now have with their religion', Sartre had ventured in his essay (an essay which is worth reading for the unintentional archaeology it provides of the roots of modern anti-Semitism), 'is as a matter of ceremonies and courtesy.' Compared to the 'strong nature' of Christianity, according to Sartre, the Hebrew religion appears at once as a 'weak' form, in the process of disintegration. Of course, when the prophet of existentialism wrote these 'strong' words, the state of Israel did not as yet exist. He can perhaps be partly excused. Now it has been in existence for over a third of a century. The Jews' prayers have become a reality; why should one not be permitted to view this reality as being an outcome, a result, of this prayer? Maybe because people are scared of finding in this prayer the fanaticism inherent in all religions — a fanaticism from which Judaism is supposed to be exempt.

There is no doubt that Rabbi Kahane provides some very strong arguments for anti-Semites of every complexion, Arabs and non-Arabs, PLO members and non-PLO members alike. In this respect he is objectively an ally of Israel's worst enemies. But the position he occupies is founded on the Torah, and on the Torah alone. It is from here that his critics are going to have to dislodge him, instead of abusing and insulting him, by the same token that our reasons for opposing Catholic dogmatism cannot simply be because it plays into the hands of its Protestant opponents.

Kahane's utterances are all the more worthy of close examination because they come at a very significant moment in Israel's history. This eloquent rabbi, who knows how to play the media, demands our attention at a moment when the realization of the dream contained in the prayer now exposes the deficiencies of the reality that has been created. The state of Israel is no longer as strong as it has led the world to believe.

Above all, when he questions the legitimacy of the state of Israel, Rabbi Kahane deliberately probes some very raw nerves. A number of key state functions in Israel — the conduct of war, the coining of money, and raising taxes — are beginning to look decidedly rickety.

1. Ever since the 1967 *Blitzkrieg*, the 'model war' which led to it being seen as the 'aggressor' in the eyes of the world, Israel can no longer wage war with the same degree of freedom. This loss of autonomy was apparent in 1973, when Golda Meir brought the country to the verge of catastrophe by not being the first to attack, and when General Sharon saw himself denied total victory over the Egyptian army. In the same way, in 1982 Israel found itself bogged down in the Lebanese quagmire because its army had no freedom of movement. 'If I had been given four

more hours,' complained General Eytan, then chief of staff, 'I could have gained total control over the road from Beirut to Damascus and the situation would have changed completely.' Why was he not granted those four hours? Because the Americans did not want to upset Syria. In short, since their famous victory in 1967, the Israelis seem to have made a mess of their wars, if not militarily then at least politically. Moreover, the invasion of Lebanon has cost the IDF much of its prestige and has greatly undermined what moral standing it had.

This loss of a few degrees of what was once a very large freedom of action has had considerable consequences, especially with regard to strategy. Up until 1967, the military doctrine prevailing in Israel was that laid down by Ben-Gurion. It consisted in hitting the enemy before he became too strong. This 'scorpion strategy' was economical of men and materials. It was a good strategy for the poor country which Israel was at the time. After 1967, having been abandoned by Europe and most particularly by Gaullist France, Israel had to look mainly to its American ally for support. And Uncle Sam was in a position to impose the defensive strategy proper to a rich country, as opposed to Israel's 'poor country' offensive strategy. Israel was thus obliged to maintain, at great cost, an absolute and costly technological superiority over its present or potential enemies — a superiority which the industrial base of its economy did not warrant. Israel was no longer permitted, or no longer permitted itself, to nip the military efforts of its enemies in the bud. This has led to a never-ending technological escalation, which is all the more expensive since arms salesmen from Britain, the US, France, etc have cheerfully taken the opportunity to supply Israel's neighbouring countries with ever more sophisticated weaponry.

This change in strategies is best reflected in the budget figures: up until 1967, the defence budget had never risen beyond 10 per cent of the gross national product. The 1967 war took it up to 18 per cent. Since then it has never fallen below 20 per cent, and between 1973 and 1976 it was consuming as much as one third of the nation's economic output. In order to understand the enormity of these percentages, one need only recall that other industrialized countries, in peacetime, devote less than 5 per cent of their GNP to defence; even the Soviet Union, which has the means to impose severe austerity measures on its population, has never been able to exceed the 14 per cent mark for its military budget, except of course during the Second World War.

Obviously, a war effort of this magnitude cannot be maintained without massive help from abroad — and that is precisely what is happening in Israel. The Americans, having proposed this strategy, also finance it. In 1985, they paid over some $3.4 billion (Israel's GNP then stood at $25 billion) — at least, that was the amount the Israelis were seeking. But the 'diplomatic price' for such aid is also high. It puts Israel's prime minister in a curious situation — a situation not without advantages, since it allows him to play Washington off against Jerusalem. On the one hand, he can use the rumblings of Jewish public opinion in order to obtain more aid from Washington; on the other, he can use directives from the White House as a justification for imposing on the Israeli population the sacrifices which are necessary to set the country's financial situation in order.

2. Despite this massive aid from the United States, Israel's war effort has created dangerous financial imbalances in another respect — by threatening the Welfare State aspect of Israel's economy: 'Welfare and Warfare', 'guns and butter'. Israel is subject to a very specific 'external constraint'. This is far more demanding than the 'external constraints' normally referred to by economists — in other words, the necessity for a country to sell to other countries as much as it buys from them in order to maintain a healthy balance of payments. In Israel's case, this external constraint — we

shall deal with it in detail later — is the necessity of maintaining a positive 'migration balance' (immigration less emigration). Were Israel to suffer an unemployment rate similar to that of other industrial countries, emigration might once again exceed immigration, as it did in 1981 (see Appendix). Hence the government's policy of keeping employment levels up, whatever the cost. This has effectively bankrupted the Israeli treasury, and has taken the inflation rate soaring to 1,000 per cent per year.

As a result, the Israeli state has printed so much money that it is no longer worth the paper it is printed on. The austerity plan of November 1984 was an attempt to stop the monetary crisis which was causing increasing numbers of Israelis to reckon their finances in dollars rather than shekels. Finance Minister Yoram Avidor even had the idea of 'dollarizing' the economy by replacing the shekel with the dollar, thus recognizing *de jure* what was already happening *de facto*.

So, we have a state which can no longer wage war with the same freedom as previously, and whose currency seems to melt away as quickly as ice cream in the Negev sun.

3. Another major state prerogative, the levying of taxes, is also being eroded in Israel. Tax evasion is now estimated at approximately 30 per cent of the state budget. In 1984, the real value of tax revenue fell by 19 per cent and 15 per cent respectively during the first and second quarters of the year. Prices were increasing at such a pace that tax payers preferred to delay paying their taxes, even if only for a month, because penalties were lower than what they could expect to gain through inflation. At this point, one could say that the state of Israel was rotting from within and the government had no choice but to step in and try to defuse this inflationary time-bomb — even at the expense of sacrificing its employment policy and thus threatening the migration balance (see above). This would see to present problems, but might possibly endanger the future.

However utopian or delirious Kahane's views may appear, they are articulated at a time when they are most likely to gain a hearing. Besides, the Jews know that one may have to pay a very high price — to say the least — for the kind of dictatorship that hyper-inflation can bring about. To say that the fundamentalist rabbi is a product of the economic and moral crises raging in Israel would be too simple; but it is also true that his violent and inflammatory language would have invited less of a following in the period when Israel could still be seen as a confident and powerful state.

Have messianic times returned? Rabbi Kahane is convinced of it. 'We are living the end of time. We are living in a messianic era. The creation of the state of Israel was just the beginning. The Messiah will come. For my part, I don't doubt it for an instant. If we are deserving of him, he may come right now, in glory and majesty. But if we don't deserve him, he'll come all the same, but in the midst of terrible sufferings. This is why I'm fighting today. I'm fighting so that the Jews become good Jews, so that there is not a catastrophe at the coming of the Messiah.'

A fortunate rabbi — come what may, he'll always be able to say: 'I told you so.'

That the Left in Israel call him a fascist, a racist and even a Nazi was only to be expected. It is also understandable that the Likud dislike him, since he is hunting on their electoral terrain and is poaching Sephardic and popular votes. Even among the extreme Right — at least as far as the leadership is concerned — the consensus is against Kahane. Why? The answers we received were all along similar lines:

Eytan: 'We disagree with Kahane because he wants to expel the Arabs.'

Levinger: 'Rabbi Kahane does not have a Jewish position. The Jews have already been driven out of many countries, and that's why, quite correctly, they don't want to inflict the same fate on the Arabs.'

Druckman: 'Because of Kahane's language and his actions, the whole world has been led to believe that we have become like the Arabs, the diametrical opposite of the Arabs. Kahane endangers the very ideas he sees himself as defending.'

Neeman: 'Kahane is an *agent provocateur*. If our enemies' intention had been to lead us astray, to have us playing into the hands of those who look for the bad in us, they couldn't have found a better way than placing Kahane in our midst so that people could call us racists, and could say that we want to drive the Arabs out. Kahane has succeeded in uniting the Arabs and the Jewish Left.'

Cohen: 'I only want to expel PLO members and those who instigate the Arabs to hatred and war against us. But not the others.'

Thus extreme Right opinions on Kahane crystallize around the rabbi's stated intention of expelling the Arabs, and their objections are similar to those of Likud and the Left. Kahane not only frightens them by giving moral weapons to the Arabs; he also leaves them with a sense of shame and tarnishes the image of Israel and Judaism in the eyes of the whole world. A man like Le Pen, supposing that he were supported by the Vatican, would provoke the same reaction among Christians. It is not Kahane's views as such that are the problem, but the fact that they are articulated by a Jew, and a rabbi at that, whose convictions are rooted in the Torah. Leading right-wing Zionists secretly fear that his attitudes will make the Jews look like Arabs. Arabs are allowed to be racists, Jews are not, because they have suffered too much from racism themselves.

But one of these leading figures has himself been accused by the press of being a racist: General Eytan. He counters in the same manner as Kahane: 'These accusations are part of the socialists' and the communists' propaganda against the Right. They call me a racist because I say what I believe. But you'll never see an Arab in a left-wing *kibbutz* or in one of their schools. Once they expelled a girl from the *kibbutz* for having married an Arab. The Left claim that they want a democratic Jewish state. But what does that mean, a democratic Jewish state? It means a state without Arabs.'

All the leaders we interviewed — for all their claims to be democrats — used the same arguments as Kahane to excuse Jewish terrorism against Arabs.

Eytan: 'We are against such terrorist attacks, but we understand the motivation behind them. The government has not come up with laws against Arab terrorism. So people take their defence into their own hands.'

Levinger: 'We have an army whose job it is to defend us. If Israelis have to resort to reprisal actions, it is their way of protesting against the lack of effectiveness of the Israeli army and the Israeli government.'

Druckman: 'The government's duty is to defend Jews. And it should pursue this energetically, so as to make Arabs scared of attacking Jews. Then the Jews would be able to move freely and safely throughout the whole of Eretz Yisrael.'

Neeman: 'We are opposed to individuals taking the law into their own hands. That's what we have a government for. What people call Jewish terrorism — I reject this term because it distorts reality — is in fact "vigilantism". When citizens of a country feel that their police force aren't doing what they're supposed to, they organize and take the law into their own hands.'

Cohen: 'They felt themselves to be undefended. They were wrong, but they were desperate.'

Not a single one of our interviewees suggested that the state might also have a duty to protect Arabs. Arabs are seen as the aggressors, whereas the Jews are only acting in legitimate self-defence — legitimate because the state is falling down in its duty. Their position is the same as Kahane's when he declares: 'We can't just sit back and watch Arabs throwing rocks at buses whenever they feel like it. They're going to have to realize that a bomb thrown at a Jewish bus is going to mean a bomb thrown at an Arab bus.' Like the others, Kahane does not openly advocate violence either, but at least he admits why: out of opportunism, in order not to give the police a reason to arrest him. Presumably the rest of the extreme Right leadership exercise a similar tactical caution.

But do they also share Kahane's position that 'no Arab is innocent'? In each case we found the same distinction between the individual Arab, whom they claim not to hate, and what one might call the 'collective Arab', who is to be suspected because he is Israel's enemy. However, none of them are for driving the Arabs out of Israel; the Arabs should be given a restricted foreign residency status, or given citizenship, provided they agree to abide by the values of the Jewish state — a rather remote probability.

General Eytan neatly sums up the position of the non-Kahanist Israeli Right in this area: 'The Arabs make up a very important minority in Israel, and we have to be on our guard with them. This minority consists of three categories. First there are the Arabs from Judea and Samaria. They are and will remain Jordanian citizens; they will never become Israeli citizens. Second, there are the Arabs who have lived in Israel since Independence and who hold Israeli identity cards. They will stay Israeli, but their rights will have to be proportional to their obligations. At present they do not do military service; therefore they cannot enjoy equal rights with [Jewish] citizens who meet all these obligations — unless they opt for some form of civilian national service. The third category consists of Arabs living in the Gaza Strip, who are neither Egyptian nor

Israeli; these Arabs should be given Jordanian citizenship.'

So there is no question of the Arabs from the first and third categories being granted the autonomous status laid down in the Camp David treaty and agreed in principle by Likud (through Begin's signature of the agreement). 'Because', says Eytan, 'autonomy for them would mean the creation of a Palestinian state, and that's what we are fighting against.' But would it be possible to annex these territories without granting their inhabitants Israeli nationality? This is the solution that Neeman favours, albeit at a later date. Twenty years from now...

But doesn't that mean setting up a sort of South African apartheid system? Our interviewees did not like this suggestion.

Eytan: 'Comparing us to South Africa means one of two things: either you don't know what you're talking about; or else you're being cheap and hitting below the belt. I cannot accept this comparison. If you want to make comparisons, look at what is happening in New York; many foreigners live there, and in particular many Jews who do not have American citizenship.'

Cohen: 'We always get the blame, whatever we do! We do not practise apartheid today, but we are already compared to South Africa. Throughout the history of the people of Israel, we have always been accused of the worst evils. Even after Begin returned Sinai, people were still blaming him for his stubbornness. We should have given back more, and more, and more... Begin returned all of Sinai, which was ridiculous, and despite that, the whole world suspected him of wanting war...'

As to Kahane, he accepts the comparison with the apartheid regime calmly, but uses it to strengthen his argument in favour of expulsion: 'I know the Arabs well and I respect them; I am convinced that not a single Arab under the age of 40 would accept such a situation.'

Rights and legal status are one thing; the demographic ratio between Jews and Arabs on Israeli territory is another.

We have already outlined Kahane's argument that the demographic prospects are threatening the very existence of the Jewish state. Our other interviewees were less pessimistic.

Eytan: 'At the time of the War of Independence [1948], there were 1,300,000 Arabs here, and 600,000 Jews. This imbalance did not prevent us from creating our state. And at that time we did not even know how many Jews would be coming to Israel.'

Druckman: 'Who had the majority here, when Zionism called on Jews to emigrate to Israel? The Arabs! The demographic problem already existed then. But the Zionists believed that the Jews would come and that they would be a majority. Theoretically the Arab population should have increased at a much faster rate since 1967, yet it is stagnating. The demographic ratio has not changed in seventeen years.'

Neeman: 'Israel is a secular and democratic state, and can quite well live with an Arab minority. Today, counting the Arabs from the West Bank and Gaza and the refugees, we have two thirds Jews and one third Arabs. So what is the problem?'

But when asked to be more concrete, they no longer deny or play down the problem. Their solution has two aspects. First aspect: if there is a demographic problem, then it will be solved by Jewish immigration. Second aspect: the Arabs must be convinced that our presence here is irreversible, in Judea and Samaria just as much as in Galilee, because they are not going to accept the existence of the state of Israel until they are convinced of this reality.

Let us deal with the *first aspect* — in other words, the way that the demographic problem might be solved by immigration or *aliyah*.

Levinger: 'Throughout the history of Zionism, there has been a demographic problem between Arabs and Jews. That is why we are pressing for a greater *aliyah*. And since I believe that the *aliyah* will increase, Jews here will become an ultra-majority. Then there will be no problem.'

Cohen: 'We won't solve the demographic problem by getting up every morning and wondering what should be done with the million Palestinians, but by asking the following question: how can we get another million Jews to come to Israel?'

Geula Cohen is very familiar with this problem; she has served as president of the *aliyah* commission in the Knesset. She doesn't think that it will be difficult to triple the influx of immigrants, provided a proper propaganda effort is made and there are suitable integration arrangements in Israel. Besides, 'Jewish history teaches us that things can change very dramatically.' (*Note:* These words were spoken at a time when, in the utmost secrecy, the Israeli government was organizing the airlift of the Falashas.)★ 'If in 1967 or 1968 you had said that 170,000 Jews would be coming from Russia, nobody would have believed you. Yet 260,000 Jews have left Russia; 170,000 came here and the rest went to the United States, because of mistakes on our part. I was against having them leave the USSR to go and live in the United States — from one Diaspora to another. Their loss is our responsibility.'

The future of the Jewish people cannot be predicted. This was one of the recurring themes during our interviews. Jews have no way of knowing what tomorrow is going to bring. As Cohen puts it: 'Our history tells us that we have to use special arithmetics. If the gates of the Soviet Union opened tomorrow, thousands, tens of thousands of Jews could end up coming here. Even in France, you have no way of knowing whether your comfortably settled neighbours might not one day think of coming here. You don't know how the coming generation are going to react, in ten years... maybe not even ten years... five years... '

Does this mean that, like Kahane, one should wish for a new wave of anti-Semitism? Our interviewees would not go that far, but they are in no doubt that the future of the state of Israel is dependent on the Diaspora returning.

Cohen: 'If there is no *aliyah*, this state has no real *raison d'être* with only three and a half million Jews. I'm not interested in this state. I didn't come here to pursue my personal salvation, or to set up a country like Greece or Switzerland. I am here to solve the problem of the Jewish people: to bring the majority of Jews to Israel.' Nahum Goldman made a 'great mistake' when he said that, in order to remain the 'salt of the world', Jews must live dispersed throughout the world. This 'mistake' is the reason that Geula Cohen cannot accept Goldman as one of the founding fathers of Israel. 'People like Goldman have always existed in Jewish history, and we are fighting against them.'

Neeman: 'The Jewish people have survived 2,000 years of suffering in the Diaspora. We believe that the Zionist solution is the only possible solution. We argue strongly for this solution. As far as we are concerned, the problem is not going to be solved until all Jews live here.'

Is the Return a divine commandment? For those of our interviewees who are believers, this is undoubtedly the case. But believers and non-believers alike agree that this argument ranks second after the main justification. Their principal justification is two-fold: Jews can live more safely inside Israel than outside Israel; and the more Jews live in Israel, the safer they will be. The Return of the Diaspora would kill two birds with one stone: both the 'Jewish' problem and the 'Palestinian' problem would be resolved.

There was little point in asking whether the Israeli economy could absorb such an influx of immigrants. The people we interviewed see Israel as a country of economic miracles. They argue that if people had looked for economic logic, the state of Israel would never have seen the light of day. And they are probably right. Each country has the economic problems it deserves or it invents for itself.

However, they forget one important point that was vital for the state of Israel: the aid that the Diaspora was able to provide not only in financial terms, but also in terms of its 'lobbying' efforts in the United States and elsewhere. Assuming that the Zionist dream becomes reality and all Jews come to live in Israel, the consequences would not only be a lower living standard (our interviewees view such a possibility with equanimity; they still dream about the heroic pioneer days of Israel's early beginnings). It would also mean losing the vitally important financial and political aid of the Diaspora. So to a certain extent we can say that God's commandment ordering the Jews to return to Israel would be self-defeating. If it ever came about, living standards in Israel would become intolerable, the state might be destroyed and the Jews would once more be dispersed...

One can also say that the Zionist commandment, even if it is only partially observed, is already self-defeating as regards its objective of having all Jews return to the Holy Land. Because the Diaspora is no longer what it used to be, due to the very existence of the state of Israel. Neeman puts it well: 'The Jews of the Diaspora are much safer now that a Jewish state exists. They are no longer the frightened Jews of before; even those who continue to live, let's say, in Mexico, own a house or have invested some money in Israel, etc... '

Our interviewees complained that Zionist propaganda has not adapted to modern means of communication; that its methods are still stuck in the nineteenth century; and that the attractions of Israel no longer have sufficient drawing-power. It may well be that Israel and the Diaspora have reached an optimal economic and political balance, but this balance could easily be upset by new disasters. On the other hand, should this balance persist, the result may be to reduce the net influx of immigrants to a few thousand per year (see Appendix); and thus Israel would be powerless to resolve the long-term demographic problem posed by the Palestinians.

This is why our interviewees envisage a *second aspect* to Israeli policy: the Arabs must be persuaded, if necessary by force, that the Jewish presence in Israel is irreversible; not until they are convinced of this will they fully accept the state of Israel.

To prove their point, our interviewees cited past experiences. What was done in Galilee, with success, they claim, must also be done on the West Bank, in other words — as official Israeli terminology would have it — in Judea and Samaria. (This terminology is justified, Neeman explained, because at the time of the British mandate, Judea was called Judea and Samaria, Samaria.)

The first thing, they claim, is that Arabs understand and respect only a policy of strength.

Levinger: 'Fraternal relations can exist between Jews and Arabs, but only if we stop the Arabs throwing molotov cocktails, stones and suchlike. We have to be tough when dealing with them.'

Eytan: 'The mentality of those who call themselves Arabs is based on the Koran. Now, you should know that the basic teaching of the Koran is that all non-Muslims are enemies. A Muslim doesn't care whether you're Jewish, Christian or something else. The Koran preaches the law of the sword. Infidels have the choice between conversion and death. This is the Koran's definition of peace. Thus, according to the Koran, there can only be peace with a non-Muslim if he becomes a Muslim or if he dies. Also, approaching the Arabs with a European mentality cannot lead, and has never led, to peace. This European mentality is diametrically opposed to their way of thinking. Therefore we must continue to be strong, and to show our strength. They are going to have to realize that they can never beat us; only then, maybe, will they change their way of seeing things.'

Hadn't their mentality already changed in Galilee? If so, why not apply the same methods in Judea and Samaria?

Druckman: 'We could talk about Nazareth, or St John of Acre, where many Arabs are living. What difference is there between Galilee and Judea and Samaria? The only difference is that Galilee has been in our hands since 1948, and Judea and Samaria only since 1967. Judea and Samaria could have been ours since 1948, and what would the difference have been then?'

Neeman: 'We had security problems in Galilee. But when the Arabs realized that we were there for good, the problems disappeared. The same goes for Judea and Samaria; until the state of Israel annexes them, thus demonstrating that their fate is sealed, the Arabs will have no reason to collaborate with us. Once they realize that we're not going to leave, they'll change their minds.'

Cohen: 'Our objective is to prevent the creation of a Palestinian state on the West Bank, by completely destroying the Palestinians' dream of ever having such a state. By establishing as many Jewish settlements as possible in Judea and Samaria, it will never again be possible to dream of having a Palestinian state there. We have already started moving in this direction, and the dream about a Palestinian state is no longer as strong as it was a while ago, with all the world supporting it. The dream of a Palestinian state has been seriously shaken by the establishment of about 150 settlements with 40,000 settlers on the West Bank. If there could be 100,000 of us there, in two to three years, then that would be even better.'

Is this any different from Kahane's position, when he

says: 'I want the Arabs to realize that, contrary to what they believe, time is not on their side.' Things have to be organized so that time is on the side of the Jews and not of the Arabs. But Kahane does not share Neeman's optimism; he does not believe that, twenty years from now, the Arabs will calmly accept the state of Israel.

By now it is obvious that, in its secular version, the solution proposed by our interviewees is in line with all the great colonial traditions. It is based on strength and numbers of people; the smaller the number of people, the greater the show of strength that is required. They have no other choice. The fact that King Hussein himself recognizes it proves that it is the right solution. He has admitted that what frightens him most is the establishment of settlements in the West Bank, since he is fully aware that this will create an irreversible situation. Jordan's head of state thus implicitly confirms the colonial rationale of the people we interviewed.

Finally, what distinguishes them from Kahane is that they believe the Arabs to be 'colonizable' sooner or later, whereas Kahane is convinced that they can never be colonized. If colonization goes hand in hand with racism, then they are far more racist than Kahane. If we agree that the course of history is firmly on the side of decolonization, then Kahane appears as far more modern and realistic than the other Zionists who, whether they admit it or not, are still imprisoned in a model of domination that has been condemned and rendered obsolete by history. In our present ideological conjuncture, Kahane seems to be right. But here again, Tehiya refers, with some justification, to the example of Galilee, which seems to have been 'forgotten' by the Arabs. Next question: does Israel actually have the financial and human resources to colonize the West Bank? This question was brushed aside by our interviewees, who reminded us of the economic miracles accomplished by the Hebrew state since its creation. It's simply a matter of will. Where there's a will, there's a way.

Geula Cohen, however, goes further in her economic argument: 'Each settlement on the West Bank has more value than a Phantom jet [*Note:* as well as costing a lot less]. Each settlement will save human lives, because it will contribute to preventing the Palestinian state from coming into existence. In my opinion, a Palestinian state will mean war. Therefore colonization means peace, since it eliminates the causes of war.

'If a Palestinian state existed in Judea and Samaria, we would not be faced with just a million enemies; there would be three or four million, coming from everywhere, from Lebanon, Kuwait, etc...

'Today we have the situation under control, because we only have to control one million of them. Granted, once in a while, they throw rocks or commit terrorist acts. But the power is in our hands. Can you imagine what it would be like with three or four million Palestinians with their guns at our throats? With the declared intention of destroying us?'

Obviously the demographic problem between Israelis and Arabs has to be viewed in the light of various political scenarios. The creation of a Palestinian state would most certainly cause a 'return' of Palestinians which the *aliyah* could never counter-balance. Given this, for the people we interviewed and for Kahane, the idea of giving up the West Bank, either wholly or in part, is out of the question. For them, Judea and Samaria are integral parts of Eretz Yisrael. 'You might as well tear out our hearts,' say Geula Cohen and Rabbi Druckman. General Eytan is convinced that the whole nation would revolt. And so on.

But supposing that this was the price for peace with the Arabs? This cannot be the price for peace, they reply, because Judea and Samaria are essential to the security and defence of Israel. Like Kahane, though, they also believe that peace with the Arabs is not a question of borders; it depends on their acceptance of the state of Israel.

But, we suggested, sooner or later these borders will have to be defined. Where will they be? The replies we were given were based on the idea of 'what we have, we hold'.

Rabbi Druckman: 'Obviously, Eretz Yisrael is much larger than the territories we have at present. But to be specific, I don't think that we should go to war to enlarge the present borders. The time will come when the whole of Eretz Yisrael will be ours. However, even before 1967, nobody here was saying that we had to fight in order to conquer Judea and Samaria. There was a war and we won. Judea and Samaria are now ours, and God forbids us to give up any part of them. It was not us who started that war. It was the Arabs. And at that time, the territories were in their hands. Consequently, anyone who comes and tells us that we are warmongers because we are building settlements in Judea and Samaria is wrong. For the very simple reason that we did not have peace before 1967, at a time when we had no settlements in Judea and Samaria. It's the Arabs themselves who give us the opportunity to conquer Eretz Yisrael. Anyway, why only go back to 1967? Let's look at what happened in 1947, when the United Nations decided to divide Eretz Yisrael. We inherited a tiny Eretz Yisrael and we accepted it. When we heard the UN's decision, we were all dancing in the streets. The Arabs, though, did not accept this decision. They went to war with us in 1948, and they lost. Afterwards they told us: "All we want is to get back the territories which you conquered in 1948. If you want peace, you must give them back." Do you think it is logical to have people forcing war and sacrifices on you, and then have them asking you to give back the territories you won in that war?'

This can be translated as follows: We did not want war. Since the war was provoked by our adversaries and not by us, they must respect the judgement of arms. It is God's judgement. The Arabs are not logical: today they promise peace in exchange for these territories — but when they had the territories, they went to war against us. Why should we trust their word today when it contradicts what they said yesterday? If we agreed to go back to the borders which existed pre-1967, by returning the West Bank, what reason have we to believe that the Arabs would not then ask us to return to the pre-1948 borders? The fact is, we have no reason to believe them. Why? Because today the Arabs are claiming the West Bank in order to create a Palestinian state. When the West Bank was still in their hands, they had the opportunity to create this state, but they didn't. Why not? Because creating such a state at that time would have implied, if not *de jure* then at least *de facto*, that they accepted the borders resulting from the 1948 war. So, if we agreed today to return to the pre-1967 borders, come tomorrow we would be obliged to go back to the pre-1948 borders.

In short: history has shown that the warmongers were the Arabs, and them alone. They appealed to the judgement of arms. And even if this judgement turns out to have gone against them, they must respect it. Those are the rules of war. War makes the rules. And war is of divine ordination.

All our interviewees, rabbis and generals alike, are true disciples of Clausewitz. To end a war, the Prussian general observed, it is not sufficient to have destroyed the enemy's forces and conquered his territories. 'Even when both these things are done, still the War, that is, the hostile feeling and action of hostile agencies, cannot be considered as at an end as long as the *will* of the enemy is not subdued also; that is, its Government and its Allies must be forced into signing a peace, or the people into submission, for whilst we are in full occupation of the country, the War may break out afresh, either in the interior or through assistance given by Allies.' (*On War*, Penguin, p. 123)

This statement fits the present situation in the Middle East remarkably well. It shows how the position taken by the far Right in Israel is simultaneously right and wrong. There will not be peace in this region until the Arabs have the 'will' for it (and one need not be a biased observer to see that this 'will' is singularly lacking). Thus Israel has good reasons not to return the conquered territories. But at the same time, one cannot rely indefinitely on the judgement of arms and on the hazards of the battlefield. Ultimately, peace is the only solution, as the God of War may not always be on Israel's side.

This is where Kahane's particular strength becomes apparent. It may be shocking for a rabbi to defend the rule of war. But if the god of that war is the same god who talked to Isaiah or to Joshua, then the thing is less shocking. Especially since God may be in favour of war just as much as of peace, victory just as much as defeat. 'There are not several messages in Judaism. There is only one. And this message is to do what God wants. Sometimes God wants us to go to war, and sometimes he wants us to live in peace. The Halacha tells us when we should make war and when we should make peace... We survived 2,000 years without a state, without an army, without power, scattered to the four corners of the world. Think of the pogroms, of Auschwitz, the concentration camps, the Inquisition — we survived all that! People who believe that we have survived all that, being atheists. are completely blind. The Jews have come back from hundreds of countries, just as the Bible said they would. We had a brilliant victory in the Six-Day War, and a few years later, during the Yom Kippur War, we lived through three terrible days. The difference between these two wars is explained by God's will... '

Some people may laugh at this statement. But the French people who answered the call of the government of the Third Republic — a very secular and democratic government — and sang a *Te Deum* at Notre Dame in Paris on the eve of Hitler's invasion will probably laugh bitterly.

Dieu et mon droit — 'God and my right'... Kahane holds no monopoly on this phrase. Does any state exist which has not been founded, implicitly or explicitly, on this formula? Strength is necessary, but it is not sufficient without the invocation of a higher authority. Call it what you will — ideology, opium of the masses or religious obscurantism — it remains as a fundamental necessity. Justice without strength, as Pascal wrote, is impotent. Strength without justice is tyranny. Justice without strength must fail, because there are bad people everywhere; strength without justice is evil. Therefore justice and strength must go hand in hand, and in order to do that, justice must be strong, and he that is strong must be just.

Jewish ideology, for its part, has a name — messianism — and once again, Kahane holds no monopoly. He comes close to the mark when he says that the Israeli Left thinks that 'it is not entirely natural for Jews to be living here in Israel'. Except that the Left are not the only ones to feel this. An 'un-natural' atmosphere has prevailed in Israel since its creation. Or, if you like, a 'miraculous' atmosphere. Isn't it natural that the Jews, who have survived 2,000 years of persecution, should believe that the realization of their 2,000-year-old dream is a miracle? The Israeli miracle started even before the creation of the state of Israel. Geula Cohen explains:

'Our dream cannot be compared to the Arab dream of restoring the past, because we have accomplished a lot. Our dream was the only way of staying alive. And those who have forgotten this dream and have left the course traced by our history have severed their ties to the people of Israel, and have assimilated. Those who continued to believe in the dream have brought it about. We are here, this is proof enough! Our dream was not a mystical dream; as a matter of fact, it was very realistic. It was aimed at one objective only: to return to Eretz Yisrael. Eretz Yisrael was on the map, right here, and not in Paradise. It was a country free from any sovereignty. This was the miracle, that 2,000 years later no one ruled over this country. It is an historical fact: neither a Palestinian nor an Arab state existed here; there have only been various empires which have appeared and disappeared.'

Why shouldn't the Return to the Promised Land, now that it has at last become a reality, herald the End of Time? 'We live in a messianic era,' Rabbi Kahane proclaims. Rabbi Levinger agrees with him: 'Everything that happens in Israel today heralds the advent of the Messiah.'

Moreover, for all its claims to be a secular movement, Zionism is, at bottom, religious.

Druckman: 'Zionism is part of the Torah. You cannot separate the two. Just as you can't say: "I believe in the Torah but not in the Sabbath." That's impossible. The Sabbath is part of the Torah, and if I believe in the Torah, I also believe in the Sabbath. And if I believe in the Torah, I also believe in Zionism.'

Thus even secular and atheist Jews remain inescapably tied to religion and to the fate of Israel.

Levinger: 'Non-religious Jews are an integral part of Israel. And according to Zionism, every Jew has his place here in Israel.'

Druckman: 'Emigrating to Israel is a religious act in itself. The thousands of people who came from all over the world saying: "We are returning home," were performing a religious act without realizing it. This act is rooted in a deep religious belief.'

This, in fact, is the specificity of Jewish messianism — the fact that it is able to be realized 'here and now', in this land promised by God, and not in some place which is beyond time and space.

Cohen: 'As a Jew you have to take upon yourself whatever misery and sacrifices are necessary for the liberation of the Jews. To a certain degree, you have to be religious to accept this. Zionism, because it is no longer a religious movement, has lost its zeal and its depth; it has lost the strength required for this struggle. Religious Jews believe that whatever they do is ordained by divine law; it gives them a great inner strength. At the beginning, to be a Zionist and to want to liberate Israel was probably enough. But once you live here, you have to take into consideration the relationship between Israel and its history. History is part of our spiritual heritage. Today everybody wonders what is the message, the meaning of the Jewish state. You have to refer to the Bible to find an answer to this question. It's true that we live like goys here. But if we sacrifice our lives, we do so because we are Jewish. What a contradiction! A young soldier who dies in Lebanon does not realize that he gives his life for the realization of his ancestors' ideals, the ideals of Greater Israel, the ideal which is written in the Bible. He believes that he is dying for the security of Israel's northern borders. He is right, but it is not enough. If you go to the bottom of the question, you understand that we give our lives for the restoration of our kingdom for which our ancestors have prayed for generations. We are links in a chain, and we have to accept all the links. If we break one of the links, we will be faced with the "why", the "how", the "until when", etc... '

Kahane uses the same image when he condemns mixed marriages, which all the other interviewees except Neeman also condemn: 'It is not only what you are doing to your own lives, but about the lives of your children, and the children of your children... It is a chain that goes far back in time and far ahead. We are all links of the same chain.'

Even an atheist like Neeman — at least he claims to be an atheist — cannot ignore the question of messianism.

For him there are two kinds of messianism: 'The first concerns the return from captivity and the restoration of the state of Israel,' he explained. 'This very pragmatic kind of messianism is Zionism. False messiahs and political movements have emerged throughout history to recreate the state of Israel. Now, at last, we have this state. It is still incomplete, but it is on the way to completion. People who believe in miracles may think that it is a miracle, and they are absolutely right. I don't believe in miracles. I believe that we succeeded in realizing part of Zionism due to a series of circumstances and of sufferings. The other messianism relates to the End of Time, the Final Judgement, when, according to the prophet Isaiah, the wolf will live peacefully with the sheep. This is utter utopia. These people believe that if we disarm, that will be an end to war. It is a dangerous kind of messianism because it is premature. It should come only as a second phase.'

This distinction is justified only if condemning pacifism is the issue. Einstein, for example, was an ardent pacifist. But, as Neeman reminded us: 'In the case of Palestine, he was in favour of fighting and winning.' And he added: 'Christians say that you should turn the other cheek. This other cheek, however, is that of a Jew! It is not their cheek. Christianity claims to be the religion of love, but it has never been brought about. And now they want the Jews to turn the other cheek.'

However, there is a way of connecting these two forms of messianism. Kahane conceives such a possibility: 'If the Jewish people act according to God's wishes, if they return to Israel, if they become as God wanted them to be, then the Messiah will come. Then there will be peace, not only in the Middle East but all over the world. There can be no peace before the advent of the Messiah.' Thus, the most rabid Zionist warriors can call themselves peacemongers, maybe even pacifists, since in fighting for Israel they are hastening the advent of the Messiah, and hence the advent of peace in the world.

Viewed in this perspective, the differences which divide Kahane from the rest of the far Right leadership in Israel seem small compared to their common fount of inspiration: 3,000 years of Jewish messianism. It would be more appropriate to call it a kind of task-sharing: one poses as a religious fanatic and by his utterances in public places articulates what the others are thinking in the secrecy of their own hearts.

All of them drink at the well of Abraham, Isaac and Jacob, because they realize that what the world now calls 'the Holocaust', however tragic it may have been, cannot be the only legitimation for the restoration of the state of Israel, even if only because the holocaust was an affair between Europeans and as such does not concern the Arabs. Therefore, they turn to God as their only other recourse.

The Messiah will come. Of that there is no doubt. His presence is already almost tangible. Nobody helped us to understand this better than Geula Cohen. When we reminded her that she had expected the Messiah to come after the creation of the state of Israel, and that she had been very disappointed when he did not come, she answered: 'I wrote this from a realistic and not from a mystical point of view. When I was in prison in Britain, I dreamed that as soon as the gates of Israel opened, all the Jews of the Diaspora would rush here to Israel. The British government, no one else, was responsible for the closing of these gates, wasn't it? Anyway, as soon as the gates opened, all the Jews would come. This was the Zionist dream. When I talked about the advent of the Messiah, it was a symbolic hope. The Messiah did not come, but to this day I haven't given up any of my dreams. And the Jewish people are waiting for the Messiah every single day. When somebody knocks at my door, I symbolically say to myself: "Maybe this is the Messiah." I even jump up, symbolically, and run to the door and say: "Maybe this is the Messiah." Even when it is the milkman, I believe that it could be the Messiah. What a wonderful life, to wait for the milkman every day, imagining that he might be the Messiah... Of course, this doesn't mean that you should take the milkman for the Messiah; otherwise you would end up in a mental hospital... Every day we dream passionately that the day will come when we shall change the world. We must be prepared to do it. And to do it, we must accept that we have to pay the price.'

Appendix:
The Demographic Issue

The demographic issue is at the heart of the controversy raised by Rabbi Kahane. Not without reason — because there is always political capital to be made from raising this particular spectre. In France, a whole series of political figures — men like Michel Debré, Pierre Chaunu and of course the far right-wing Jean-Marie Le Pen — have stirred people's fears by comparing the declining birthrate of the French with the high birthrate among the immigrant population.

What do the statistics tell us? If we look at present-day Israel, not counting the Occupied Territories of the West Bank, the rabbi's fears appear to be justified, even when official statistics are taken as a reference.

a) The birthrate of non-Jews (34.7%) clearly exceeds that of Jews (22.4%). Over the past twenty years, both have fallen sharply. However, at the start of the period, the birthrate of non-Jews was very high (50.3%).

b) The growth rate of the non-Jewish population (3.2% per year) is also higher than that of Jews (1.9%), as shown in Table I. In the case of non-Jews, this rate has remained stable, whereas it is tending to fall for Jews.

These growth rates have been computed so as to include immigration (331,000 Jews between 1972 and 1983). Now, as Table I shows, the yearly influx of immigrants is falling drastically (55,000 per year at the start of the 1970s; 18,000 in 1983). In 1981, the figure for emigration actually exceeded that for immigration.

c) Israel's total population between 1961 and 1983 increased from 2,179,500 to 4,148,500, a multiplication factor of 1.9; during the same period, the non-Jewish population grew from 247,100 to 712,500, a multiplication factor of 2.9 (Table II).

d) As a result of these trends, the overall percentage of non-Jews, which had fallen during the 1950s, has been growing continuously during the past twenty years and, according to latest official figures, has reached 17.1%.

e) According to official forecasts, the percentage of non-Jews will reach *at least* 22% by the year 2000.

f) Table III shows that Ashkenazi Jews are now a minority within the Jewish population in Israel.

If one now adds the Arab population of the West Bank, estimated at 1.3 million, as an integral part of Israel, the ratio of non-Jews to Jews changes completely: approximately 37:63.

This ratio is relatively stable (or so Yuval Neeman claims), since the Arab population of the West Bank has remained stable, and because of its statistical weight this stability has its effect on the other elements of the demographic equation. But this is only a hypothesis.

First of all, there is no reason to think that West Bank Arabs have a different birthrate to Israeli Arabs; the population of the West Bank would therefore only remain stable if this high birthrate were counterbalanced by an equally high emigration to Arab countries (Jordan, Kuwait, United Arab Emirates, etc). This would be plausible, since the Israelis try very hard to encourage such an exodus, but there are no firm statistics which enable one to measure this trend.

In any case, the stability of this ratio depends largely on

developments in the political situation. If the West Bank were to become the Palestinian state that the PLO dreams of, it is extremely likely that this demographic balance would be overturned. For the Israelis, this is yet one more argument — in addition to strategic considerations — for not accepting such a state. However, the demographic ratio would also be upset if the Arabs of the West Bank were to be fully integrated into Israeli citizenship in the event of there being a properly ordered annexation. In this case, Israel could easily find itself with a 40% Arab population. To deny these figures as a figment of Rabbi Kahane's ravings would be to ignore the facts of the situation.

Many of the people we interviewed would prefer to see the problem solved by a massive *aliyah*. Not even the most optimistic Israeli statistics envisage such a possibility (Table II). Unless Israel can revert to to the immigration levels of the 'miraculous years', the demographic rise of the Arabs is not going to be effectively counterbalanced by an *aliyah*, particularly at a time when unemployment in Israel is soaring and living standards are declining.

Besides, the evolution of the Jewish population throughout the world bears out Israeli statistics. According to official figures (Table IV), the world Jewish population has stagnated over the past ten years, mainly because of the low Jewish birthrate, but also because of the mixed marriages which Kahane so abhors. Shortly before his death, Nahum Goldman told us that today's Jewish population would have reached 100 million if it had not been for so many mixed marriages.

There are reasons to believe that the world's Jewish population is beginning to decrease. In the face of this trend, how could immigration possibly regain its former strength? Unless, of course, another disaster were to befall the Jewish people...

Chronology

1881: A series of deadly pogroms struck the Jewish communities in Romania and Russia. Many Jews fled to Palestine. They called themselves the 'lovers of Zion'.

1885: The Dreyfus affair. A correspondent of the Vienna *Neue Freie Presse* was covering the trial of the Jewish captain in Paris. He conceived the idea of a Jewish state. His name was Theodor Herzl.

1914: Chaim Weizmann, a Russian-born chemist living in London, discovered a revolutionary method for producing the acetone required to manufacture explosives. Because of his invention, he was in contact with many leading personalities of the British establishment, which enabled him to propagate the theses of Zionism.

2 November 1917: Lord Balfour, secretary of state at the Foreign Office, wrote in a letter to Lord Rothschild that: 'His Majesty's government views with favour the establishment in Palestine of a national home for the Jewish people and will use their best endeavours to facilitate the achievement of this object, it being clearly understood that nothing shall be done which may prejudice the civil and religious rights of the existing non-Jewish communities in Palestine, or the rights and political status enjoyed by Jews in any other country.' President Wilson of the United States gave his support to what history now knows as the 'Balfour

Declaration'. The American head of state declared: 'I am convinced that the Allies, with the total support of our government and of our nation, will accept that the foundations for a "Jewish Commonwealth" are established in Palestine.'

16 September 1922: The League of Nations ratified the Balfour Declaration by giving Britain mandate powers over Palestine. However, on 22 June, Winston Churchill, then secretary of state for the colonies, told the House of Commons, as a means of reassuring the Arabs, that 'Great Britain had no intention of making a Jewish state of Palestine.' Conflict immediately broke out between Jews and Arabs. The Zionists created a clandestine army, the Haganah.

August 1929: The Jewish Agency was created in Zurich, with the intention of buying land in Palestine and organizing the emigration of Jews to Israel.

1939: The Chamberlain government published a White Paper fixing upper limits on Jewish immigration to Palestine, and imposing strict regulations on land sales.

1939–45 War: The British government moved to ban immigration. Ships were sent back and sunk, while fighting began again between Jews and Arabs. Haganah organized clandestine immigration, and the Irgun resorted to direct attacks on British forces, including, subsequently, the bombing that destroyed the King David Hotel, the British forces HQ in Jerusalem.

30 November 1947: The General Assembly of the United Nations voted in favour of partitioning Palestine into two states, one Jewish and the other Arab, forming an economic union, while Jerusalem and Bethlehem were to become international zones.

14 May 1948: Eight hours after the termination of the British mandate, David Ben-Gurion proclaimed the state of Israel.

15 May 1948: Five Arab armies invaded Israel. The United States recognized the state of Israel *de facto*; the USSR followed suit on 17 May.

7 January 1949: End of the war, with Israel having increased its territory by 30 per cent. Jordan annexed the west bank of the River Jordan (West Bank). Upwards of 750,000 Arabs fled to neighbouring states.

26 July 1956: Gamal Abd el-Nasser nationalized the Suez Canal.

29 October 1956: Beginning of the Suez war. With the support of French and British forces, the Israeli army advanced rapidly towards the Canal. Under pressure from the two superpowers, the French and British armies withdrew, followed by Israel.
UN forces assigned to guard strategic areas on the Israeli-Egyptian border.

19 May 1967: Having convinced the UN to withdraw its troops, Nasser blockaded the Gulf of Aqaba.

5–10 June 1967: Israel launched a 'pre-emptive' war. Within six days, Israel had occupied Sinai, the Golan Heights and the West Bank, including East Jerusalem.

10 June 1967: The USSR broke off diplomatic relations with Israel.

22 November 1967: UN Security Council Resolution 242★ was passed unanimously.

6 October 1973: During Yom Kippur celebrations, Egypt crossed the Suez Canal and invaded Sinai, while Syrian forces attacked the Golan Heights.

October–December 1973: Price of oil quadrupled.

4 September 1975: After two years of negotiations, an 'interim' agreement was signed in Geneva.

17 May 1977: Menachem Begin formed a conservative coalition government, ending the long ascendancy of the Labour Party.

19 November 1977: Sadat visited Jerusalem.

1979: Camp David agreement between Begin and Sadat, under the aegis of President Carter.

June 1982: Israel invaded Lebanon.

February 1985: First stage of withdrawal of Israeli army from southern Lebanon.

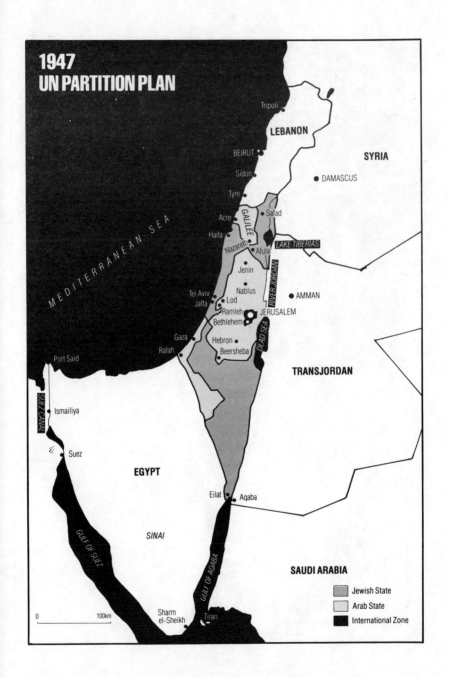

1947
UN PARTITION PLAN

Tripoli

LEBANON

BEIRUT

SYRIA

Sidon

DAMASCUS

Tyre

Acre

GALILEE

Safad

Haifa

Nazareth

Afula

LAKE TIBERIAS

MEDITERRANEAN SEA

Jenin

RIVER JORDAN

Tel Aviv

Nablus

Jaffa

Lod

AMMAN

Ramleh

JERUSALEM

Bethlehem

DEAD SEA

Gaza

Hebron

Rafah

Beersheba

Port Said

TRANSJORDAN

SUEZ CANAL

Ismailiya

Suez

EGYPT

Eilat

Aqaba

SINAI

GULF OF SUEZ

GULF OF AQABA

SAUDI ARABIA

Jewish State

Arab State

International Zone

0   100km

Sharm el-Sheikh

Tiran

181

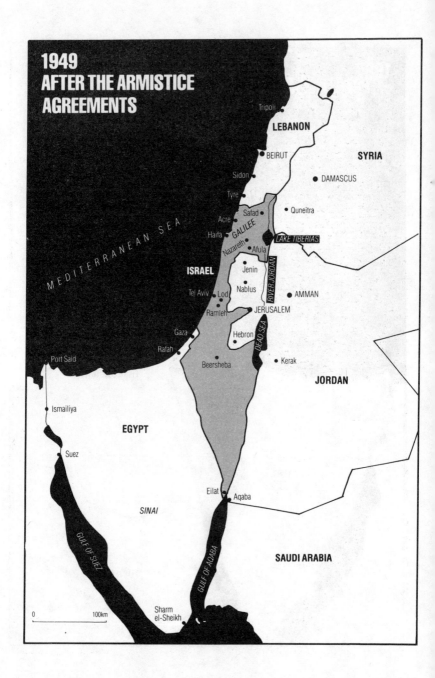

1949
AFTER THE ARMISTICE
AGREEMENTS

MEDITERRANEAN SEA

Tripoli

LEBANON

SYRIA

BEIRUT

Sidon

● DAMASCUS

Tyre

Acre · Safad · · Quneitra

Haifa **GALILEE**

Nazareth · Afula *LAKE TIBERIAS*

ISRAEL

Jenin *RIVER JORDAN*

Tel Aviv · Lod Nablus

Ramleh · · AMMAN

JERUSALEM

Gaza · Hebron *DEAD SEA*

Rafah

Port Said · Beersheba · Kerak

JORDAN

Ismailiya

EGYPT

Suez

Eilat · Aqaba

SINAI

SAUDI ARABIA

GULF OF SUEZ

GULF OF AQABA

0   100km

Sharm
el-Sheikh

182

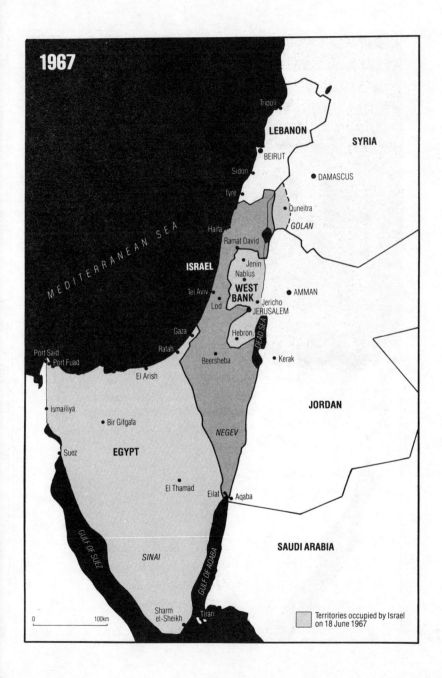

183

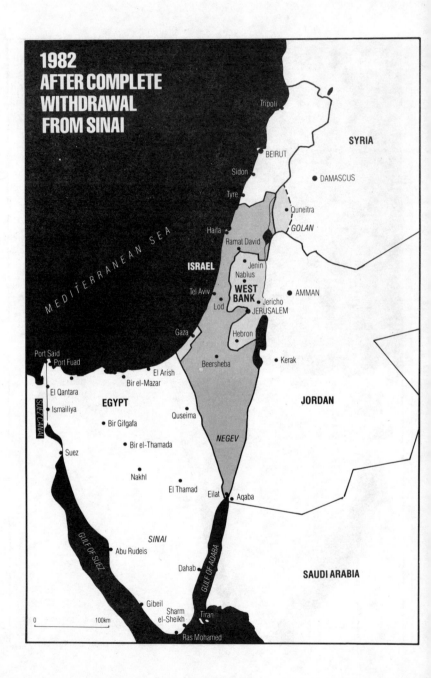

1982
AFTER COMPLETE
WITHDRAWAL
FROM SINAI

SYRIA

Tripoli

BEIRUT

Sidon

DAMASCUS

Tyre

Quneitra

GOLAN

Haifa

Ramat David

MEDITERRANEAN SEA

ISRAEL

Jenin

Nablus

Tel Aviv

WEST BANK

AMMAN

Lod

Jericho

JERUSALEM

Gaza

Hebron

Beersheba

Kerak

Port Said

Port Fuad

El Arish

Bir el-Mazar

El Qantara

JORDAN

Ismailiya

EGYPT

Quseima

SUEZ CANAL

Bir Gifgafa

NEGEV

Suez

Bir el-Thamada

Nakhl

El Thamad

Eilat

Aqaba

SINAI

Abu Rudeis

Dahab

GULF OF SUEZ

GULF OF AQABA

SAUDI ARABIA

Gibeil

Sharm el-Sheikh

Tiran

Ras Mohamed

0   100km

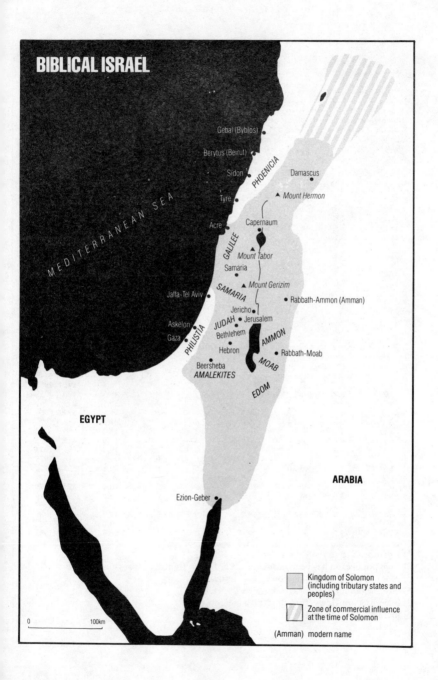

BIBLICAL ISRAEL

MEDITERRANEAN SEA

Gebal (Byblos)

Berytus (Beirut)

Sidon

PHOENICIA

Damascus

Tyre

▲ Mount Hermon

Acre

Capernaum

GALILEE

▲ Mount Tabor

Samaria

SAMARIA

▲ Mount Gerizim

Jaffa-Tel Aviv

Rabbath-Ammon (Amman)

Jericho

Askelon

JUDAH

Jerusalem

Gaza

PHILISTIA

Bethlehem

AMMON

Hebron

Rabbath-Moab

Beersheba

MOAB

AMALEKITES

EDOM

EGYPT

ARABIA

Ezion-Geber

Kingdom of Solomon
(including tributary states and
peoples)

Zone of commercial influence
at the time of Solomon

(Amman) modern name

0   100km

TABLE I

Population growth in Israel

Share of net immigration in total growth	Yearly growth rate	Population at end of period	Total growth	Immigration	Migratory balance	Natural growth of period	Population at start	
8 = 3:5	7 = 5:1	6 = 1 + 5	5 = 2 + 3	4	3	2	1	
Jews								
60.1	6.2	2,662.0	2,012.4	..	1,207.0	805.4	649.6	1948-71[1,2]
90.3	26.5	1,203.0	553.4	..	499.6	53.8	649.6	1948-50[2]
52.2	4.6	1,911.2	708.2	..	369.7	338.5	1,203.0	1951-60
45.0	2.4	2,662.0	750.8	..	337.9	412.9	1,911.2	1961-71
24.7	2.1	3,436.1	774.0	331.0	191.6	582.0	2,662.0	1972-83
50.6	3.4	2,752.7	90.7	55.4	45.9	44.8	2,662.0	1972
52.1	3.4	2,845.0	92.3	54.2	48.0	44.2	2,752.7	1973
20.4	2.2	2,906.9	62.0	31.3	12.7	49.3	2,845.0	1974
1.2	1.8	2,959.4	52.5	19.7	0.6	51.8	2,906.9	1975
11.5	2.0	3,020.4	61.0	19.5	7.0	53.9	2,959.4	1976
12.2	1.9	3,077.3	56.9	21.3	7.0	50.0	3,020.4	1977
26.1	2.0	3,141.2	63.9	26.8	16.7	47.2	3,077.3	1978
38.2	2.5	3,218.4	77.2	37.2	29.5	47.7	3,141.2	1979
25.6	2.0	3,282.7	64.3	20.5	16.5	47.8	3,218.4	1980
..	1.1	3,320.3	37.5	12.7	−10.2	47.7	3,282.7	1981
9.1	1.6	3,373.2	52.9	14.1	4.9	47.9	3,320.3	1982
20.8	1.9	3,436.1	62.9	18.2	13.1	49.7	3,373.2	1983
Non-Jews								
..	3.2	191.8	35.8	..	..	35.8	156.0	1948-54[2]
0.9	4.3[3]	458.7	266.9[6]	..	1.8	196.4	191.8	1955-71
0.2	3.7	239.2	47.4	..	0.1	47.3	191.8	1955-60
4.2	4.6	299.3	60.1	..	2.5	57.7	239.2	1961-65
..	4.5[3]	458.7	159.4[6]	..	−0.6	91.4	299.3	1966-71
2.4[5]	3.8[5]	712.4	259.0[5]	22.8	6.0	241.1	453.6	1972-83
2.6	4.1	472.3	18.7	2.2	0.5	18.2	453.6	1972
9.2	4.4	493.2	20.9	2.3	1.9	19.0	472.3	1973
7.4	4.4	514.7	21.5	2.2	1.6	19.9	493.2	1974
..	3.7	533.8	19.1	1.8	−0.3	19.4	514.7	1975
1.9	3.8	555.0	21.2	1.6	0.4	20.8	533.8	1976
1.9	3.8	575.9	20.9	1.5	0.4	20.5	555.0	1977
0.3	3.5	596.4	20.5	1.9	0.1	20.4	575.9	1978
1.7	3.6	617.8	21.5	2.4	0.4	21.1	596.4	1979
4.6	3.4	639.0	21.2	1.7	1.0	20.2	617.8	1980
..	2.9	657.5	18.7	1.9	−1.2	19.9	639.0	1981
0.3[2]	3.2[4]	690.4	32.9[3]	2.0	0.1	20.9	657.5	1982
5.6	3.2	712.4	22.0	1.3	1.2	20.8	690.4	1983

1) As from 15 June 1948
2) 1948 population has been estimated according to figures for previous periods
3) Not including the population of East Jerusalem
4) Not including non-Jews from the Golan Heights
5) Including non-Jews from the Golan Heights
6) Including East Jerusalem.

Tables

TABLE II

Demographic Pattern
(Not including the Occupied Territories)
(in '000 inhabitants)

	Total population	Jewish population	Non-Jewish population as %
(Nov.) 1948	872.7	156.0	17.9
1961	2,179.5	247.1	11.3
1972	3,147.7	461.0	14.6
1980	3,921.7	639.0	16.3
1981	3,977.9	675.5	16.5
1982	4,063.6	690.4	17.0
1983	4,148.5	712.5	17.1

Forecast for year 2000

Hypothesis A:	5,339.6	1,212.8	22.8
Hypothesis B:	5,504.1	1,212.8	22.0

Hypothesis A: net immigration of 5,000 per year
Hypothesis B: net immigration from 1980 to 1990: 15,000 per year; 5,000 per year from 1990 to 2000

TABLE III

Israel's Jewish population in 1983,
viewed by country of origin (in '000s)

Total	3,404.6
● born in Israel	1,994.7
with father from:	
– Europe/America	563.6
– Africa	428.5
– Asia	448.59
– Israel	553.5
● born outside Israel	1,409.9
– Europe/America	783.1
– Africa	331.9
– Asia	294.9

TABLE IV

*The Jewish population
worldwide (in '000,000s)*

1882	8
1900	11
1914	14
1925	15
1939	16
1948 (15 June)	11
1955	12
1970	13
1975	13
1980	13
1982	13

Glossary

Aliyah: From the Hebrew word meaning 'to ascend'; a Jew 'makes his *aliyah*' when he emigrates to Israel.

Altalena: Name of the ship carrying a secret shipment of arms for the Irgun, and which Ben-Gurion ordered to be surrounded; the Haganah opened fire on Begin's partisans. This was the first mortal conflict among the Jews of Palestine before the creation of the state of Israel. A second instance was to follow, when the pacifist militant Emil Grunzweig was killed by a member of an extreme right-wing Jewish terrorist group.

Ashkenazis: Literally 'German' Jews; Jews of European origin, as opposed to *Sephardis*.

Bar Kokhba: A Jew who resisted the Romans; honoured and sometimes criticized for having propagated and carried out a war to the death against the Romans.

B'nai B'rith: Literally 'Son of the Alliance'. An American organization with branches in Europe; it had freemasonic and secular characteristics, and its objective was to obtain equal rights for the Jews. Freud was a member of this group.

Bney Brak: A small town near Tel Aviv, inhabited by Orthodox Jews not necessarily hostile to the Jewish state, but refraining from participation in public life.

Cabala: The traditional and most common term for the esoteric teachings of Judaism and for Jewish mysticism, especially in the forms it assumed in the Middle Ages.

Camp David: Camp David agreement signed in 1979 by Begin representing Israel, Sadat representing Egypt, and Carter representing the United States. Under this agreement, a peace treaty was concluded between Egypt and Israel on the basis of the restitution of Sinai, and negotiations between Israel, Egypt and Jordan for the establishment of 'autonomy' for West Bank Palestinians. The latter part of this agreement was never applied.

Cohen: The name given to temple priests (an alternative version is Kahane). People carrying this name are supposed to be the descendants of priests.

Declaration of Independence: Israel's independence was declared on 14 May 1948, by Ben-Gurion. The Declaration of Independence contains a number of principles which are the foundations of the Jewish state. The declaration first restates the Jewish people's historic right to Palestine: 'The land of Israel is the place where the Jewish people was born, and it was here that it formed its spiritual, national and religious identity.' Then the declaration appeals to the Jews of the Diaspora to return to Israel, this option being open to them under the Law of Return. It proclaims the democratic principles which Israel will respect: 'It [the Jewish state] will be founded on the principles of freedom, justice and peace which were taught by the prophets of Israel; it will guarantee full freedom of conscience, worship, education and culture... ' As regards the Arab population of Israel, the declaration invites them to share fully in the life of the state, on the basis of full citizenship.

Development towns: Newly created towns in Israel, mainly populated by Sephardic Jews; they are less prosperous than other large Israeli towns.

Diaspora: From the Greek word meaning 'dispersion';

designates Jews who live outside of Israel. There have been two diasporas in the history of the Jewish people: the first in Babylon after the destruction of the first Temple (sixth century BC) and the second, still in operation today, after the destruction of the second Temple in AD 70. These constitute the two major exiles of the Jewish people.

Eretz Yisrael: Literally 'Land of Israel', the Hebrew name given to the state of Israel. Some foreign reporters and the nationalist parties extend this term to include Greater Israel.

Falashas: Black Jews from Ethiopia who for centuries have lived on the fringes of world Judaism and who only follow the Torah, rather than the Talmud. Their origins are obscure. According to legend, they are supposed to be descendants of Menelik, an offspring of King Solomon and the Queen of Sheba. The Grand Rabbinate of Israel recognized them as Jews in 1973, and declared them to be descendants of the tribe of Dan. A more serious hypothesis, albeit not yet verified, claims that they are descendants of the Agau people converted to Judaism 2,500 years ago by a Jewish garrison on the island of Elephantine, near the modern Aswan. Operation Moses in 1973 airlifted 6,000 of them out of Ethiopia, bringing their total in Israel to 13,000.

Goy: Literally meaning 'people'; term by which Jews designate non-Jews.

Haganah: A Jewish self-defence organization created during the time of the British mandate. Its members fought with the British against the Nazis, but later turned against them. The largest of all the para-military organizations, the Haganah was also the most moderate. It made up the backbone of the Israeli army that was set up after 1948.

Halacha: The doctrine, rules and laws of Judaism, codified into juridical law.

Hanukkah: An eight-day Jewish holiday commemorating the victory of the Maccabeans and the purification of the Temple; it is symbolized by a chandelier with eight branches, one of which is lit each evening.

Hellenists: A derogatory term designating Jews who are attracted by foreign cultures. Historically, it stems from the conflicts in the Mediterranean basin between Jewish culture and Greek culture, the latter having devastated many Jewish communities, including the one at Alexandria.

Herut: A party founded in 1948 by former members of the Irgun, and headed by Menachem Begin. Herut supports the notion of a Greater Israel, and of economic liberalism. It makes up the backbone of the Likud right-wing coalition.

Histadrut: Israel's general federation of labour.

Irgun: Extremist armed terrorist group set up in 1935 by Palestinian Jews David Rasiel and Abraham Stern (who later left it, to create the group that was to bear his name). Inspired by extreme right-wing revisionist Zionism, it refused to take the pressure off the British during World War II. It was responsible for numerous attacks on the British and the Arabs, and was dissolved after the assassination of the UN mediator Count Bernadotte in September 1948.

Isaiah: Jewish prophet (eighth century BC) who lived at the time of the Assyrians' victory over the Kingdom of Israel. He preached the almightiness of God, and repudiated materialism and militarism; he announced the universal Kingdom of the Messiah.

Israel: This term, denoting the Jewish people, was the name given by God to Jacob when he overcame an angel sent by God. Literally translated, Israel means 'contended with God'.

Jericho: A town on the West Bank near the Dead Sea in the Jordan Valley. The first town conquered by the Hebrew people when they penetrated the Promised Land, headed by Joshua. The walls of the town tumbled down at the sound of Joshua's trumpet.

Joshua: Lived at the end of the twelfth century and the start of the eleventh century BC. He was chief of staff to Moses, whom he succeeded in order to lead the Hebrew people to the Promised Land or Canaan.

Kibbutz (pl. *kibbutzim*): Collective village operating in principle without private property. There are 230 in Israel (2 per cent of the population). Many were set up at the time of the Zionist pioneer era; they also played a military role. Today, agricultural activity in the *kibbutzim* goes hand in hand with industrial enterprise; the basic rules of the *kibbutzim* are often disregarded nowadays, with the use of paid labour. The *kibbutzim* have become prosperous.

Knesset: From the term Beth-Knesset, meaning 'synagogue'. This is the name given to Israel's single-chamber parliament. The Knesset has 120 deputies, elected nationally on the basis of proportional representation. This form of voting means that small parties can also be represented. The eleventh Knesset elected in July 1984 comprised no less than fifteen parties. The following is a list of the parties, giving the number of their MPs and their percentage of the national vote (in brackets):

  – Left coalition (Labour and Mapam): 44 (34.9)
  – Likud: 41 (31.9)
  – Tehiya: 5 (4)
  – NRP (National Religious Party): 4 (3.5)
  – Hadash (communist grouping): 4 (3.4)
  – Shas (religious, Sephardi): 4 (3.1)
  – Shinui (centre Left): 3 (2.6)
  – Movement of Civil Rights (Left): 3 (2.4)
  – Yahad (Ezer Weizman's new Centre party): 3 (2.2)
  – Progressive List for Peace (Left, Arab voters and Jewish-Arab list): 2 (1.8)
  – Agudat Israel (religious): 2 (1.7)
  – Morasha: 2 (1.6)
  – Tami (Sephardi): 1 (1.5)

- Kach: 1 (1.2)
- Ometz (independent): 1 (1.2)

Kosher: Term for the foods authorized under Jewish law.

Maimonides: Jewish theologian, philosopher and doctor (1135-1204). Lived in Spain before fleeing from the Inquisition. Wrote several treatises on philosophy and theology, such as the *Guide of the Lost.* Considered by many to be the most important Jewish philosopher, he was a convinced rationalist.

Mapai: Jewish social-democratic party created in Palestine in 1930. Has dominated Israeli political life since that time, and headed all governments up to 1977. Founded by Ben-Gurion. In 1968, Mapai fused with Ahdut Ha'avodah (Yigal Allon's socialist party) and Rafi (formed after a split in the Mapai provoked by Ben-Gurion) and became the Labour Party.

Mapam: United Workers' Party, founded in 1948. An extreme left-wing party. Has for a long time maintained close ties with the international communist movement. Its members sing the Internationale and carry red flags when they march. This party has 'quietened down' to a certain extent, and has participated in government coalitions together with the Labour Alignment, under the name of Maarak. Mapam, which has a marked pacifist line, refused to take part in the National Unity government in 1984.

Mea Shearim: Or 'hundred gates', the ultra-Orthodox section of Jerusalem. Its inhabitants do not recognize the existence of the state of Israel and believe that the Jewish national renaissance can only be the work of the Messiah.

Messiah: Literally meaning 'anointed'. An envoy who will be sent by God to bring universal peace and the resurrection of the dead. The Messiah will rebuild the Temple.

Mezuzah: A small scroll inscribed with Jewish scriptural writings: 'Hear, O Israel, the Lord our God is One God.' It is enclosed in a small holder which in Jewish tradition is fixed to the doorposts of houses, stores, offices and all religious sites.

Moshav (pl. *moshavim*): Cooperative farm with privately owned land.

Omar and El Aqsa Mosques: Two of the most sacred sites of Islam. They are located in Jerusalem on the Temple Mount, the exact site where the Jewish Temple was built and the location of the Ark, the 'Holy of Holies'. Thus the mount is also the most sacred site of Judaism. According to Jewish tradition, it will be the Messiah who will rebuild the Temple.

Oz Veshalom: 'Fortitude and Peace'; movement of 'dovish' rabbis.

Rabbi: A man qualified to judge in civil law and religious matters and recognized as such by the community. In present times, this title is obtained after religious studies. It is now a full-time function.

Resolution 242 of the Security Council: Voted by the UN's Security Council after the Six-Day War. It calls for Israel to withdraw from occupied territories in exchange for a just and lasting peace with its Arab neighbours. It is contested by the PLO because it deals with the Palestinians as merely a refugee problem. Israel refers to the English text, which speaks of withdrawal from 'territories', whereas the French text reads 'les territoires' (the territories).

Sabbath: The seventh day, on which God rested after having created the world. Starting on Friday evening and ending on Saturday evening, this is a holy day for Jews. They have to observe a day of total rest; in particular they are not to light fires. Respect of the Sabbath is one of the most important commandments of the Torah.

Sabra: Any Israeli citizen born in Israel.

Sanhedrin: High Court in ancient Palestine. Within the religious economy of Judaism, it had the power to make decisions in all political, social, religious and juridical matters. It had seventy members and was presided over by a *nasi* (prince). It represented the Jews against the Romans, and had its seat within the grounds of the Temple. Ceased to exist after AD 70 when the Temple was destroyed.

Saul: First Hebrew king proclaimed by Samuel the prophet. He founded a kingdom of warriors.

Sephardis: Oriental Jews; literally meaning 'Spanish' Jews and referring to their origins. They came from Arab countries and the Mediterranean basin. They constitute more than 60 per cent of Israel's Jewish population.

Shalom Akhshav: 'Peace Now', a loosely structured Israeli pacifist movement fighting for the restitution of Palestinian territory in exchange for peace. It was able to organize a 400,000-strong demonstration in Tel Aviv after the Sabra and Chatila massacres.

Stern Gang: Extremist terrorist movement opposing the British mandate. Created from a split with the Irgun.

Talith: Prayer shawl.

Talmud: Literally meaning 'instruction'. A compilation including the Mishnah, which in turn is a compilation of rabbinical commentaries and decisions on the Torah. A complete instruction in Jewish social and religious life, containing arguments on all points. There are two Talmuds: one, called the Jerusalem Talmud (completed in the fourth century), and the other the Babylonian Talmud, more complete, and written in Aramaic between the fourth and fifth centuries, and the most widely used. The Talmud is a compilation of law and oral traditions.

Torah: The Pentateuch (five books), ie the first part of the Hebrew Bible. It contains God's commandments as handed down to Moses.

Tsahal: Israel Defence Force (IDF), the name of Israel's army.

Yarmulka: Skull-cap used by religious Jews, covering their heads in deference to God.

Glossary

Yeshiva: High school for Talmudic studies.

Zionism: From Mount Zion in Jerusalem. A political movement which started at the end of the nineteenth century, and works for Diaspora Jews to return to what is now Israel.

Index of Names

Index